MW01098136

ASHE Higher Education Report: Volume 40, Number 3
Kelly Ward, Lisa E. Wolf-Wendel, Series Editors

Black Male Collegians: Increasing Access, Retention, and Persistence in Higher Education

Robert T. Palmer

J. Luke Wood

T. Elon Dancy II

Terrell L. Strayhorn

Black Male Collegians: Increasing Access, Retention, and Persistence in Higher Education
Robert T. Palmer, J. Luke Wood, T. Elon Dancy II, Terrell L. Strayhorn
ASHE Higher Education Report: Volume 40, Number 3
Kelly Ward, Lisa E. Wolf-Wendel, Series Editors

Cover image by © Mustafahacalaki/iStockphoto.

ISSN 1551-6970   electronic ISSN 1554-6306   ISBN 978-1-118-94165-2

The ASHE Higher Education Report is part of the Jossey-Bass Higher and Adult
Education Series and is published six times a year by Wiley Subscription Services,
Inc., A Wiley Company, at Jossey-Bass, One Montgomery Street, Suite 1200, San
Francisco, California 94104-4594.

Individual subscription rate (in USD): $174 per year US/Can/Mex, $210 rest of
world; institutional subscription rate: $327 US, $387 Can/Mex, $438 rest of world.
Single copy rate: $29. Electronic only–all regions: $174 individual, $327
institutional; Print & Electronic–US: $192 individual, $376 institutional; Print &
Electronic–Canada/Mexico: $192 individual, $436 institutional; Print &
Electronic–Rest of World: $228 individual, $487 institutional. See the Back
Issue/Subscription Order Form in the back of this volume.

CALL FOR PROPOSALS: Prospective authors are strongly encouraged to contact
Kelly Ward (kaward@wsu.edu) or Lisa E. Wolf-Wendel (lwolf@ku.edu). See "About
the ASHE Higher Education Report Series" in the back of this volume.

Visit the Jossey-Bass Web site at **www.josseybass.com.**

The ASHE Higher Education Report is indexed in CIJE: Current Index to
Journals in Education (ERIC), Education Index/Abstracts (H.W. Wilson), ERIC
Database (Education Resources Information Center), Higher Education Abstracts
(Claremont Graduate University), IBR & IBZ: International Bibliographies of
Periodical Literature (K.G. Saur), and Resources in Education (ERIC).

Advisory Board

The ASHE Higher Education Report Series is sponsored by the Association for the Study of Higher Education (ASHE), which provides an editorial advisory board of ASHE members.

Contents

Executive Summary

Improving college access and success among Black males has garnered tremendous attention. For example, there have been policy reports from the College Board Advocacy and Policy Center and the Center for the Study of Race and Equity in Education at the University of Pennsylvania. Furthermore, there are a number of journals, such as *Journal of African American Males in Education, Challenge Journal: A Journal of Research on African American Men, Spectrum: A Journal on Black Men*, among others, devoted to scholarly inquiry and providing insight into the experiences, conditions, and challenges facing Black males in education and beyond. At the same time, many educational researchers have sought to provide critical insight and have raised thought-provoking questions about Black males through peer-reviewed articles and books.

The focus on Black males is warranted. Many social scientists have noted that Black men account for 4.3% of the total enrollment at four-year postsecondary institutions in the United States. Incidentally, the percentage of Black men who are enrolled in college is the same as it was in 1976. According to national data, two thirds of Black men who start college never finish. The educational challenges of Black men have caused major concern among stakeholders in higher education. From this concern emerged a number of empirical studies, policy reports, journals, retention programs, and books focused on ways to help improve educational outcomes among Black male collegians. This monograph was conceived with a similar goal in mind. Specifically, the monograph provides a comprehensive synthesis and analysis of literature on factors promoting the access, retention, and persistence of Black men in post-secondary education. One of the key components of the monograph is its focus on the experiences of Black men in diverse institutional contexts (i.e., historically Black colleges and universities, predominantly White institutions, and community colleges). This approach recognizes the institutional heterogeneity of colleges and universities in America's higher education system as well as the diverse student characteristics and experiences within those contexts. By employing this approach, this monograph realizes that adopting a "one size fits all" method is not the most practical way to help improve the plight of Black men in higher education. The monograph includes recommendations and strategies to help advance success among Black males relative to the diverse institutional contexts of focus.

The monograph consists of four chapters. In the first chapter, we provided a justification for this monograph by discussing the underachievement of Black men throughout the educational pipeline. Keeping consistent with the aim of this monograph, we contextualize the academic achievement of Black men within the diverse institutional types of focus in this monograph. The first chapter is critical because it provides a foundation to help understand some of the challenges that Black men experience as they progress through the educational pipeline. In the second chapter, we highlight the preK–12 experience of Black men, focusing specifically on factors that restrict or limit their participation in higher education. In the third chapter, we discuss programs and policies that help to facilitate access to higher education for Black men; more so, we also examine critical factors to their retention and persistence. Finally, in the fourth chapter, we discuss implications for research, policy, and practice. Given its unique approach and comprehensive focus, this monograph is an important resource for faculty, administrators, and staff in preK–12 and postsecondary education. The monograph will also be rendered valuable by educational policymakers. Additionally, we surmise this monograph will be deemed a useful resource for scholars, institutional researchers, and graduate students who are interested in pursuing empirical research in this critical line of inquiry.

Dedications

Robert T. Palmer would like to dedicate this monograph to his mentors and friends in the academy, who have inspired him to be resilient and focused on succeeding in every endeavor. J. Luke Wood would like to dedicate this monograph to his son, J. Luke Wood, Jr., you inspire me toward excellence. T. Elon Dancy would like to dedicate this monograph to his mentees and the vast numbers of Black boys and men who endeavor to realize their dreams in U.S. educational institutions. Terrell L. Strayhorn would like to dedicate this monograph to all those motivated to excel in their respective endeavors, whose commitments and passions encourage, inspire, and fuel me daily.

Foreword

Readers do not need to venture far in the popular press, social media, or political commentary to find topics related to African American men in U.S. society. Topics range from concern for Black men, the plight of urban youth, and getting beyond stereotypes. And, of course, there has been considerable attention to the narrative and rhetoric related to the often cited statement by President Obama (who at the time of the statement in 2007 was a senator) indicating "we have more Black men in prison than we have in our colleges." The statement, though untrue, triggered considerable attention to many of the issues that face African American men. The attention generated by the statement highlights concerns about Black men in higher education including access, affordability, and completion. These concerns have led to interest and subsequent research related to different aspects of the representation and performance of African American men in colleges and universities.

The monograph, *Black Male Collegians: Increasing Access, Retention, and Persistence in Higher Education* coauthored by Robert T. Palmer, J. Luke Wood, T. Elon Dancy II, and Terrell L. Strayhorn, examines the recent spate of research related to different aspects of higher education for Black men. The monograph is comprehensive in its review of current research and practice. In an increasingly diverse landscape of higher education and society in general, the number of Black men participating in higher education has not changed considerably in the past 30 years. Topics in the monograph explore the many books, articles, and reports that look at the experiences of Black men in higher education. The monograph has a twofold purpose—to highlight the experiences of Black men in the diversity of higher education contexts and to look at the factors that promote access, retention, and persistence. The authors present information that clearly articulates and outlines problems associated with underachievement and underrepresentation of Black men in higher education *and* clearly summarizes the strategies that help promote success.

In a field of study that has rapidly increased, it is often difficult to find a key source that integrates and provides an overall picture of the topic at hand. Research related to Black men in higher education has increased so rapidly, making it hard for readers to keep up. The monograph is a key resource to summarize and analyze the burgeoning and diverse areas of research and practice. As a researcher, I am generally interested in topics related to diversity and student success, but I have not focused on topics related to Black men. Reading the monograph provided me with a compendium of information to get an overall understanding and clear articulation of current issues related to African American men in higher education. The monograph provides an understanding of the current status of Black men in different sectors of education (preK–12 and higher education) as a way to encapsulate the pipeline of (under)achievement through education and in different educational settings. The authors also provide a synthesis of current research related to programs and policies that promote access and success. Readers looking for a synopsis of topics related to Black men in higher education will find a solid base of information. Researchers interested in more in-depth topics will also find the authors' synthesis and analysis comprehensive and a useful tool to provide a foundation for future research about Black men in higher education and related topics.

Authors Palmer, Wood, Dancy, and Strayhorn join a complementary collection of other ASHE monograph topics that look at different aspects of diversity. For example, *Latinos in Higher Education*; *Immigrant Students in Higher Education*; *Postsecondary Education for American Indian and Alaska Natives*; *Asian Americans in Higher Education*; *Stonewall's Legacy: Bisexual, Gay, Lesbian, and Transgender Students in Higher Education*; and *Allies for Inclusion: Disability and Equity in Higher Education* all examine current research and practice looking at other underrepresented groups in higher education. In addition we've included more general topics related to diversity such as *Engaging Diversity in Undergraduate Classrooms* and a forthcoming volume on critical race theory. The intent is for researchers and practitioners to read these monographs alone or collectively as a way to grasp current research and practice to further success for all students.

There are no easy answers or one size fits all responses to the Black male "crisis" in higher education. Instead, practitioners and policy makers need to be informed about the realities and complexities of African American men in all aspects of higher education and in different educational contexts. The monograph admirably synthesizes current research as a way to clarify the situation and provide promising practices to give practitioners and researchers new and different ways to think about Black men in higher education.

Kelly Ward
Lisa E. Wolf-Wendel
Series Editors

Acknowledgments

Robert T. Palmer: I would like to note that it was an honor working with the coauthors of this monograph. These men are extremely humbled, but yet so talented and passionate about promoting success for Black men in education. I would also like to thank J. Oscar Simmons for helping me to realize that tomorrow holds a promise for a better, more prosperous day.

J. Luke Wood: I would like to acknowledge my cocontributors whose scholarly contributions have been essential to advancing the field of Black male studies in education. I would also like to acknowledge my colleague, Frank Harris III, for his support and mentorship.

T. Elon Dancy II: I thank my coauthors for their dedicated work, colleagueship, and community. I am always indebted for the support of a very loving family, particularly my mother, Gwendolyn. In addition, I value the mentors, colleagues, and friends who sustain me as I continue in this work. Finally, I am thankful for Zawadi who teaches me daily about love and its possibilities.

Terrell L. Strayhorn: I would like to acknowledge all those involved in advancing scholarship on Black males in education, including my coauthors. I would also offer sincere thanks to the members of my research team and staff in the Center for Inclusion, Diversity & Academic Success (IDEAS) at The Ohio State University. Constant support and encouragement from my son and daughter, lifelong friends, and family make all of my work possible.

Published online in Wiley Online Library
(wileyonlinelibrary.com) • DOI: 10.1002/aehe.20015

Contextualizing the Experiences of Black Men in Society and Education: Setting the Foundation

I N THE PAST DECADE, there has been a heightened awareness of issues facing boys and men of color in society. Once overlooked, discourse
on issues concerning these individuals (particularly those of Black/African
American descent) has been elevated in the scholarly community and among
practitioners. With respect to the prior, the scholarly community has wit-
nessed a rapid expansion of publication venues and works specific to Black
boys and men. Beginning with the *Journal of African American Men* in 1995
(later renamed the *Journal of African American Studies*), the foundations for
publication outlets specific to the Black male experience were made. Since
then, additional journals have been founded, including: *Challenge Journal:
A Journal of Research on African American Men* (2007); *Journal of African
American Males in Education (JAAME)* (2010); *Journal of Black Masculinity*
(2010); and most recently, *Spectrum: A Journal of Black Men* (2012). The latter
(*Spectrum*) is a particularly salient addition to the fold, as its establishment
represents the first instance (to our knowledge) of a university press—Indiana
University Press—featuring a journal specific to the lives and experiences of
Black men.

In line with the expansion of peer-reviewed outlets, conference presentations and publications on Black boys and men have also been on the rise.

Among higher education academicians, the focus on Black men has risen, particularly in the past three years. Conference presentations at the Association for the Study of Higher Education (ASHE)—the leading scholarly society of researchers in the field of higher education—serve as a barometer of an enhanced focus on the collegiate realities of Black males. For example, 10 years ago, the ASHE conference held in Portland, Oregon, in 2003, featured only one presentation focused explicitly on Black males in postsecondary education. This presentation titled "Home, School, and Community Factors that Influence African-American Males to Attend College" was presented by James Coaxum and Donavan McCargo (2003). Between 2004 and 2010, approximately five presentations per year focused on Black males in higher education. In 2011, the Council on Ethnic Participation, an affiliated council of ASHE dedicated to enhancing participation among ethnic minorities in ASHE, established a preconference forum. Since then, the number of presentations on Black men has doubled, with the 2012 conference in Las Vegas even featuring four symposia on Black men (see Table 1; Appendix). This growth of scholarly presentations on Black men is impressive and is not representative of the exponential growth of research being presented at NASPA, American College Personnel Association (ACPA), and the Council for the Study of Community Colleges among others.

Corresponding to an increase in conference presentations, the number of peer-reviewed works on Black boys and men has grown exponentially. Hundreds of peer-reviewed studies have focused on Black males in colleges and universities (though only a handful appear in the leading "mainstream" higher education journals). Numerous subgenres have emerged, focusing on Black men by institutional type (e.g., predominantly White universities, historically Black colleges and universities, community colleges); level (e.g., undergraduate, graduate); identity (e.g., gender, sexual orientation); academic status (e.g., gifted education, underprepared); involvement (e.g., Greek life, athletic participation); and millennial students. As noted, one sector of this literature has focused on Black men enrolled in community colleges. The growth of literature in this subgenre elucidates the wider trend in the field. Wood and Hilton (2012a) conducted a synthesis of research on African American

TABLE 1
ASHE Conference Presentations on Black Men

	2003 Portland	2004 Kansas City	2005 Philadelphia	2006 Anaheim	2007 Louisville	2008 Jacksonville	2009 Vancouver	2010 Indianapolis	2011 Charlotte	2012 Las Vegas	2013 St. Louis
GC–Symposium	–	–	–	–	–	1	–	1	–	3	–
GC–Paper	1	1	4	2	3	3	2	1	3	–	5
GC–Roundtable	–	–	1	1	1	–	–	3	5	2	1
GC–Poster	–	2	1	–	–	3	1	–	2	–	2
CEP–Symposium									–	1	–
CEP–Paper									2	1	1
CEP–Roundtable									–	5	–
CEP–Poster									–	–	–
Total	1	3	6	3	4	5	3	5	12	12	9

Notes: GC: General Conference; CEP: Council on Ethnic Participation. CEP preconference was established in 2011.

Source: The above table was created from an analysis of the ASHE conference programs based on presentation titles.

males in the community college. One of the first peer-reviewed works on Black males in community colleges was published in 1998 in the *Community College Journal of Research and Practice*. This article, authored by Harold Mason, presented an initial empirical model on Black urban male persistence using a small sample of men from Chicago. Since then, more than 20 additional peer-reviewed works have been published, 14 in the last three years. In addition to these works, numerous academic book chapters and reports are in accompaniment (Minority Male Community College Collaborative, n.d.).

In addition to peer-reviewed works, numerous books on Black males in postsecondary education have proliferated in the past several years (with several books in press). These books address a multiplicity of topical areas relevant to Black men in colleges and universities, they include *Academically Gifted African American Male College Students* (Bonner, 2010); *African American Men in College* (Cuyjet, 2006); *Advancing Black Male Student Success From Preschool Through Ph.D.* (Harper & Wood, in press); *Black Men in College: Implications for HBCUs and Beyond* (Palmer & Wood, 2012); *The Brother Code: Manhood and Masculinity Among African American Men in College* (Dancy, 2012); *Black Males in Postsecondary Education: Examining Their Experiences in Diverse Institutional Contexts* (Hilton, Wood, & Lewis, 2012) among others. The authors of this monograph have been intimately involved in advancing research on Black males, both in the ASHE community and among scholars in our respective research sectors (e.g., student affairs, community colleges, masculinities). As contributors to this greater research literature on Black men via numerous publications and research studies, we have become attuned to emergent themes emanating from the growing field of Black males in postsecondary education. Recurrent themes among these works often provide rationales for investigating the Black male postsecondary reality. Such justifications are centered on three core notions, that (a) Black men occupy a sociopolitical–historical space in American history that is unique and that manifests acute challenges to success; (b) Black men are both racial and gendered beings that have distinct socialization experiences that influence how they navigate, interpret, are perceived, and received by educational institutions; and (c) Black men often exist on the margins of post-secondary student life yet have stories of resistance, triumph, and resiliency that can inform educational programming, policies, and practices for *all* students.

Purpose of the Monograph: Reshaping the Puzzle

As evidenced by the increase of academic journals, conference presentations, peer-reviewed articles, and books on Black men in college, the field has grown dramatically in recent years. Numerous researchers have engaged in scholarly inquiry on challenges and opportunities facing Black men in college. This research has resulted in a body of literature that addresses a broad array of topics, utilizes diverse methodological approaches, presents compelling findings, and provides practical recommendations for policy and practice. In general, the nature of social science research is complex. Therefore, elucidating meaning and understanding of social phenomena affecting Black males is often difficult and tedious work, as multiple (and sometimes competing) factors can influence student outcomes. Thus, gaining clarity in social inquiry requires rigorous empirical and conceptual efforts on behalf of social scientists. Each phenomenon examined (i.e., Black male persistence, sense of belonging, identity development) is akin to a puzzle in which numerous researchers with varied methodological tools add pieces to create a more comprehensive view of the larger picture.

Over time, a mountainous volume of scholarship can contribute to researchers losing sight of the larger puzzles being examined. Inevitably, until scholars become refocused on the larger puzzle, two issues will take place: (a) duplication of research will occur whereby studies unnecessarily explore questions for which numerous scholars have already found warranted assertions; and (b) missing pieces will be overlooked in areas in desperate need of exploration or more in-depth analysis is left unaddressed. The result of these two outcomes will produce the same result, incomplete puzzles for research and limited direction for practice. Ultimately, it is our intention that this monograph serves to add context to this puzzle by synthesizing what is known and what needs to be known about Black men.

Methodological Approach: A Modified Literature Synthesis

As noted by Bland, Meurer, and Maldonado (1995) and Patterson, Thorne, Canam, and Jillings (2001), there is a need to periodically synthesize research literature, in any given field, in order to apprise academicians and practitioners on the condition of the field. While much research has focused on the Black male experience in various educational contexts and provided critical insight for increasing their participation and success in postsecondary education (Cuyjet, 1997, 2006; Dancy, 2012; Dancy & Brown, 2012; Harper, 2006a, 2012; Palmer, Davis, & Hilton, 2009; Palmer & Wood, 2012; Strayhorn, 2008a, 2009, 2010; Wood, 2012; Wood & Turner, 2011), the purpose of this monograph is to develop a comprehensive synthesis and analysis of literature on factors promoting the access, retention, and persistence of Black men in higher education. Our goal is to provide a comprehensive understanding of the status of the literature and offer "fresh" suggestions on new/revised areas for future inquiry.

In this monograph, we synthesized research on Black men in college using a modified literature metasynthesis approach. Literature metasynthesis is a process by which multiple types of studies (e.g., quantitative, qualitative, mixed-methods, conceptual) are collected and synthesized for emergent themes (Patterson et al., 2001; Turner, González, & Wood, 2008). Specifically, we reviewed existing articles, books, book chapters, policy briefs, and reports focused on this population to construct and compose a much needed sourcebook that delineates institutional policies, programs, practices, and other factors that encourage or hinder the retention and persistence of Black men in postsecondary education. Additional works were identified using multiple search engines (e.g., Google Scholar, ERIC, ProQuest, Springer Collection, Project Muse, DOAJ) as well as available university library systems. From an exhaustive search, hundreds of articles and other publication types (e.g., books, book chapters, reports, policy briefs, news articles) were identified for review. The majority of the literature review is presented in the second and third chapters of this monograph while the fourth chapter serves to convey insights from the process as well as suggestions for future research. In presenting findings from our review of the literature, we organize our presentations around institutional types, with a specific focus on historically Black college and universities (HBCUs), predominantly White institutions (PWIs), and community colleges. We do so given that the overwhelming majority of Black men are enrolled in these institutional types; moreover, the bulk of research on these men is focused on these institutional contexts.

To set the stage for the subsequent chapters in this monograph, the remainder of this chapter is dedicated to overviewing the status of Black males in preK–12 and in American postsecondary education. But first, we clarify our use of the terms "Black" and "African American." Based on our extensive review, these terms are often used interchangeably in the scholarly literature (Berhanu & Jackson, 2012; Billie & Carter, 2012; Palmer & Davis 2012; Terry, 2010; Wood & Hilton, 2012a). In a more specific sense, the term African American has also been employed to refer to those who are of African descent and living in the United States (Cashmore, 2004) as well as more specifically to generational descendants of African slaves living in the United States (Wood, 2008). Generally, the term Black is used in the literature to refer to all peoples of African descent in the United State regardless of historical lineage, generation status, or country of origin (Cashmore, 2004). That being said, some of the data sources and studies cited throughout this monograph employ differing definitions that may be more or less restrictive. However, we will primarily employ the term Black throughout this monograph, without specific attention to the nuances between these terms. We do so, as the term Black is a more inclusive term, portraying a perspective of a common Black identity.

Snapshot: Black Males in PreK–12 Education

In this section, we briefly highlight some factors relevant to the experience of Black males in preK–12 education. A more extensive treatment of precollegiate considerations is offered in the second chapter. Our research, as well as that of other scholars in the field, has often sought to provide a sociohistorical context to understanding why institutions of higher education fail Black men. Informed by the work of Estela Bensimon (2004, 2005, 2007) on equity and institutional accountability, we purposely situate the responsibility for Black male achievement on the institutions that serve them. In contrast to this perspective, much of the literature and practice regarding Black boys and men has employed a deficit framework (see Harper, 2012), blaming them, their families, and their communities for inadequate enrollment and success outcomes (Wood & Essien-Wood, 2012). Bush and Bush (2004) challenged the deficit framework by using the parable of a tree bearing fruit, with the tree being a metaphor for an institution and the fruit representing students. They noted that "good" institutions will bear good fruit (positive student outcomes) while bad institutions produce the opposite. They employ this imagery to illustrate the importance of holding institutions accountable for effective practices and outcomes.

Institutions of higher education are "rooted" in and affected by larger structural-environmental contexts. Specifically, postsecondary institutions are merely microcosms of a society "rife with contradictions and asymmetries of power and privilege" (McLaren, 2003, p. 69). As such, race and racism have been central to shaping the experiences of Blacks in America, serving as an inhibitor to their upward mobility (DeCuir & Dixson, 2004). Blacks in general (and particularly Black men) have historically served to fuel the underclass in American society as "slaves, sharecroppers, tenant-farmers, maids, Pullman porters, factory workers and others at the base of bourgeois society" (Ferguson, 2011, p. 69). Indeed, they occupy a unique social position that is typified by a lack of power and privilege (Wood & Essien-Wood, 2012), often attributable to the confluence of racism and classism. For example, racism, particularly in the form of racial microaggressions (small, subtle racial slights), has a direct effect on how Black men encounter, navigate, and engage educational institutions (Ingram, 2013).

Beginning in early childhood education, subtle stereotypical messages regarding the cognitive abilities, behaviors, and life expectations for Black males are received from teachers, peers, and the media (Davis, 2003). These messages convey to them that they do not belong and that they are not capable of succeeding in academics. As a result, Black boys are socialized in early education to lack self-confidence and a sense of belonging in school (Baggerly & Max, 2005). This circumstance is further influenced by the lack of diversity among preK–12 teachers. The vast majority, 90%, of teachers are White, and the overwhelming majority of these are female (National Collaborative on Diversity in the Teaching Force, 2004). Thus, Black boys often do not see or engage with individuals in positions of school authority who look like them. This can further exacerbate Black boys' assessments of the utility of and their belonging in school. Moreover, Lewis, Simon, Uzzell, Horwitz, and Casserly (2010) noted that the majority of Black boys are educated in urban schools. These institutions, in comparison to their suburban counterparts, have higher levels of unqualified, inexperienced, and uncertified teachers (Humphrey, Koppich, & Hough, 2005; Marnie, 2002; Porter & Soper, 2003; Rowland & Coble, 2005); higher teacher turnover rates (Education Commission of the States, 2003); and (more often than not) operate with dilapidated resources and outdated facilities (Cortese, 2007).

Another deleterious influence on how Black boys are treated in school comes from the media. In the media, Black males are often depicted as gangsters, drug dealers, and street thugs. These images characterize Black males as aggressive, nefarious, indolent, ignorant, and brutish. Even positive depictions of Black men are typically restricted to portrayals of entertainers and athletes. These media images overwhelmingly paint Black males as lacking morality and being intellectually inferior (Wood & Hilton, 2013). As a result, Black boys are often treated as such in school. The overrepresentation of Black males in exclusionary discipline and in special education alludes to these perspectives (Darensbourg, Perez, & Blake, 2010).

Black males are overrepresented in exclusionary discipline (e.g., detention, suspension, expulsion, school replacements). Prior research suggests that exclusionary discipline serves as a socializing pathway in routing Black males toward the criminal justice system (Darensbourg et al., 2010). Data from Lewis, Butler, Bonner, and Joubert (2010) shed light on exclusionary practices. They collected data from an urban school district in the Midwest to investigate differences in discipline responses to Black and White male students. They found that while Black males made up only 11% of the total district population, they accounted for almost 37% of all disciplinary sanctions. Most of the behavioral infractions were for disobedience (47%) and defiance (17%) as opposed to fights, threats, or thefts (15% combined). However, of the total percent of male students assigned to behavioral sanctions, they represented 33% of detentions, 38% of in-school suspensions, 37.9% of out-of-school (three-day) suspensions, and 38.5% of out-of-school (five-day) suspensions. Their study serves to illuminate a larger trend evident at the national level. For example, 49% of Black males in public middle through high schools have been suspended at some point. This is the highest rate among any other racial/ethnic and gender group. In comparison, only 21% of White males have been suspended in these grades (National Household Education Surveys [NHES], 2007).

Along with exclusionary discipline, special education serves as another aspect of education where the influence of societal perceptions of Black males is evident. Interestingly, prior data have shown that White school districts label greater percentages of Black males as having disabilities (Ladner, 2007). Similarly, research has also shown that the percentage placement of Black males in special education is positively correlated with the percentage of White teachers in a school (Herrera, 1998). For example, in the state of Arizona, at schools that are less than 25% White, the representation of students with learning disabilities, emotional disorders, and mental retardation is 14.1%, 8.4%, and 7.5%, respectively. However, in schools where the student body is more than 75% White, those rates edge up to 15.5%, 9.2%, and 11.6%. In contrast, White males at those same (primarily White) schools are represented with disabilities as follows: learning disability (8.1%), emotional disturbance (2.6%), and mental retardation (1.3%). These data represent significant percentage gaps in the representation of Black and White males in special education (Ladner, 2007). At the national level, the overrepresentation of Black males in special education is also evident. Perhaps most egregious, Black males (in and of themselves) account for 20% of all students labeled as mentally retarded (National Education Association, 2011). Clearly, these data indicate that some mislabeling is occurring. The data in this section as a whole indicate just a few of the numerous challenges facing Black males in preK–12, where they are exposed to experiences that can mar their trust in educational institutions and educators. With the above in mind, the next section provides an overview of the enrollment and outcome data on Black men in postsecondary education.

Status: Black Men in Postsecondary Education

Obtaining a college degree is widely viewed as an important benefit to society (e.g., increased economic tax base, reduced reliance for social services, enhanced civic engagement) and to oneself (Futrell, 1999; Levinson, 2007; Vernez & Mizell, 2001). Nevarez and Wood (2010) indicated that there are multiple individual benefits to a baccalaureate education, they include enhanced career mobility and security, social networks, employment skills, professional standing, and consumer savvy. Likely, these benefits are also attributable to postbaccaluareate degree attainment. Chief among the benefits of a college education is the increased earning potential associated with a postsecondary degree. For instance, a Black male can expect to earn $30,723 a year with a high school diploma alone; however, with a bachelor's degree their mean earnings rise to $55,655 (an increase of nearly $25,000 per year). An increase in earnings is also seen for those Black men who earn master's degrees, with mean earnings of $68,890 (an increase of roughly $13,000 from a bachelor's degree per year). While these data illustrate the tangible significance of achieving successive levels of education, it should be noted that the economic benefits of a degree differ by race. White men reap higher mean earnings per year than their Black male counterparts. A White male with a high school diploma will earn $5,695 more per year than a Black male with the same degree ($36,418 per year). Greater disparities are seen at successive degree levels, where White men with bachelor's and master's degrees earn $15,631 ($71,286 per year) and $22,886 ($91,776 per year) more than Black men, respectively (U.S. Census Bureau, 2012).

Blacks have a long history of valuing education (Allen, Jewell, Griffin, & Wolf, 2007; Palmer et al., 2009). Black males enroll in colleges and universities with the goal of enhanced social and economic mobility (Bush & Bush, 2010). However, enrollment data shed light on disconcerting patterns of underrepresentation and gender disparities (Dancy & Brown, 2008; Jackson & Moore, 2006, 2008; Palmer & Maramba, 2012; Palmer & Wood, 2012; Strayhorn, 2008a, 2009, 2010).

College and University Enrollment

Many social scientists have noted that Black men account for 4.3% of the total enrollment at four-year postsecondary institutions in the United States (Harper, 2006a, 2012; Palmer & Strayhorn, 2008; Strayhorn, 2008a, 2010). Incidentally, the percentage of Black men who are enrolled in college is nearly the same as it was in 1976 (Harper, 2006a; Palmer & Strayhorn, 2008; Strayhorn, 2008a, 2010). For example, data from the Digest of Education Statistics (2011a) indicate that Black male students accounted for only 5.18% of total postsecondary enrollment. This is a particularly concerning percentage given that college-age Black men (ages 18–54; this age range may seem large, but is inclusive of men who attend community colleges) accounted for 6.24% of the population among this age bracket (U.S. Census Bureau, 2000). Disparate patterns are more readily apparent when viewed at the undergraduate and postbaccalaureate levels. Among undergraduates, Black men accounted for 4.57% of the general undergraduate population in 1976. More than three decades later, their representation has risen by less than one point (0.86% to be exact) to 5.43%. In comparison to their female counterparts, Black men have long been underrepresented at the collegiate level. Black women have outpaced Black men in undergraduate enrollment, a trend that continues to rise over time. While the percentage difference between Black men and women was only 0.87% in 1976, the percentage gap rose to 3.93% in 2010.

The dismal representation of Black men in college is even more apparent at the postbaccalaureate level. In 1976, Black males represented only 2.50% of postbaccalaureate enrollees in degree-granting institutions. This percentage remained stagnant for more than two decades, with an uptick to 3.61% in 2010. Though Black men accounted for 3.61% of the total postbaccalaureate population, Black women represented 8.71% (a difference of 5.10%; see Table 2). In all, the aforementioned data illustrate two primary points. First, Black men are underrepresented at the collegiate level in comparison to their total proportion in the general college-age population. Second, Black women

TABLE 2
Percentage of Black Males and Females Among Enrollees in Degree-Granting Institutions

	1976	1980	1990	2000	2010
Black male undergraduate (%)	4.57	4.09	3.74	4.38	5.43
Black female undergraduate (%)	5.44	5.64	5.84	7.38	9.36
% Difference	−0.87	−1.55	−2.10	−3.00	−3.93
Black male postbaccalaureate (%)	2.50	2.19	1.97	2.70	3.61
Black female postbaccalaureate (%)	3.22	3.23	3.39	5.70	8.71
% Difference	−0.72	−1.04	−1.42	−3.00	−5.10
Black male total (%)	4.27	3.83	3.50	4.14	5.18
Black female total (%)	5.12	5.31	5.51	7.15	9.27
% Difference	−0.85	−1.48	−2.01	−3.01	−4.09

Source: Digest of Education Statistics. (2011a). *Higher Education General Information Survey (HEGIS), "Fall Enrollment in Colleges and Universities" surveys, 1976 and 1980; Integrated Postsecondary Education Data System (IPEDS), "Fall Enrollment Survey" (IPEDS-EF:90); and IPEDS Spring 2001 through Spring 2011, Enrollment component.* Washington, DC: U.S. Department of Education, National Center for Education Statistics.

are enrolled at the undergraduate and postbaccalaureate level at higher rates than their male peers, a trend that has and continues to expand.

The aforementioned data are presented with a general focus on postsecondary education; however, there is wide variation in enrollment patterns and experiential realities by institutional type (see Hilton et al., 2012). Table 3 presents the percentage of undergraduate men enrolled in postsecondary education by race and institutional sector. These data illuminate variation in enrollment characteristics by institutional type. Specifically, of the total percentage of Black undergraduate men, 41.0% are enrolled in public two-year institutions (commonly referred to as community colleges). Given these data, Bush and Bush (2010) have noted that community colleges serve as the primary pathway into postsecondary education for Black men. In contrast, only 33.2% are enrolled in public and private not-for-profit four-year colleges and universities (with the majority of those in public colleges, 23.1%). Interestingly, while the largest proportion of Black male collegians are enrolled in community colleges, the vast majority of literature on Black men in

TABLE 3
Percentage of Men by Race Enrolled in Postsecondary Education by Sector

Institutional Sector	Public Four-Year	Private Not-For-Profit Four-Year	Public Two-Year	Private For-Profit	Others or More Than One
Total	30.4	11.7	39.2	10.8	7.9
Black	**23.1**	**10.1**	**41.0**	**18.6**	**7.3**
White	32.8	13.3	37.3	8.7	7.9
Latino	25.3	7.1	46.6	12.9	8.1
Asian	38.1	12.6	34.0	6.7	8.6
American Indian or Alaska native	26.0	6.1	36.9	21.6	9.4
Native Hawaiian/ other Pacific Islander	27.7	9.2	45.2	9.0	8.8
Other	28.8	13.9	39.9	9.9	7.5

Source: National Postsecondary Student Aid Study. (2012a). *NPSAS institution sector (4 with multiple) by race/ethnicity (with multiple) for gender (male)*. Washington, DC: U.S. Department of Education, National Center for Education Statistics.

postsecondary education focuses on their experiences and outcomes in four-year colleges and universities (Wood, 2013; Wood & Turner, 2011).

Interestingly, a large contingent of Black male collegians, 18.6%, are enrolled in private for-profit colleges and universities. This is an increased distribution, given that in 2004, only 12.0% of Black men were enrolled in for-profit colleges (NPSAS, 2004). This distributional percentage is larger than all groups, other than Native American/Alaskan Indian males (at 21.6%). This is a particularly concerning percentage given that prior research has shown that for-profit colleges attendees pay higher tuition (Miller & Mupinga, 2006; Riegg, 2006), incur greater loans (Mullin, 2010), are more likely to default on their loans, and have higher levels of unemployment (U.S. GAO, 2011) than public institutions. Specific to men of color, Wood and Vasquez Urias (2012) used national data from the Beginning Postsecondary Student's Longitudinal Study to compare satisfaction outcomes for men of color in community colleges and for-profit colleges (proprietary schools). They found that men of color attending public two-year colleges had higher levels of program

TABLE 4
Black Male Enrollment in HBCUs by Institutional Level and Control, Fall 2010

	Total	Public Four-Year	Public Two-Year	Private Four-Year	Private Two-Year
Total number	101,644	65,552	7,116	28,904	72
Percent	100%	64.49%	7.0%	28.43%	<1%

Source: Digest of Education Statistics. (2011b). *Integrated Postsecondary Education Data System, "Fall Enrollment Survey" (IPEDS-EF:90); Spring 2001 and Spring 2011, Enrollment component; Spring 2011, Finance component; and Fall 2010, Completions component.* Washington, DC: U.S. Department of Education, National Center for Education Statistics.

satisfaction, satisfaction with the cost-effectiveness of their degree, and perceptions of degree quality, than those attending for-profit institutions.

Considering the challenges associated with for-profit attendance, it is important to note that Black men are more likely than their White and Asian male counterparts to attend for-profit colleges. For example, only 8.7% of White and 6.7% of Asian male undergraduate enrollment is dispersed into the private for-profit sector. Moreover, the opposite trend is evident for enrollment at public four-year institutions. A greater proportion of White and Asian undergraduate enrollment is concentrated in public four-year colleges. The distribution of White and Asian male enrollment is 9.7% and 15.0% greater than the distribution of Black men (at 32.8% and 38.1%, respectively; NPSAS 2012a).

Finally, while institutional types can be examined based on the level (e.g., two-year, four-year) and control (e.g., public, private for-profit, private not-for-profit), there is another distinguishing characteristic directly relevant to this monograph's focus on men of Black descent. While there are more than three million Black men enrolled in colleges and universities around the nation, more than one hundred thousand (101,644 to be exact) are enrolled in institutions that are designated as HBCUs (see Table 4). HBCUs are defined by federal law as colleges and universities with a mission focus on serving African Americans that were established prior to 1964 (Lee, 2012). There are a total of 105 HBCUs in the nation serving over 300,000 students; these institutions are diverse, ranging in size, religious affiliation (e.g., religious, nonsectarian), and enrollment selectivity (Gasman et al., 2007). Consistent with the fact that most HBCUs are four-year institutions, the majority of Black male enrollees (64.5%) are at public four-year HBCUs though 28.4% are enrolled at private not-for-profit HBCUs (Table 4).

In totality, the aforementioned data on enrollment by institutional type convey several key considerations. First, the distribution of Black men by institutional sector indicates that public two-year colleges serve as their primary avenue of access into postsecondary education. Second, a sizeable distribution of Black men are enrolled in for-profit colleges; based on prior data, a trend of increasing enrollment in this sector is apparent. Third, in comparison to the White and Asian male peers, Black men are more likely to be distributed in public two-year colleges and for-profit colleges, but less likely to be distributed in public and private not-for-profit four-year colleges and universities. Fourth, HBCUs serve as a critical institutional type that provides a large level of access to postsecondary education for Black men. As an aside, it is important to note that there is a dearth of literature on Black men in for-profit colleges and universities. In fact, at the time of this writing, only one scholarly work (see Fountaine, 2012) has an explicit focus on this population. As such, the treatment of this segment of the Black male collegiate population is not addressed in this monograph (since this monograph is a synthesis of extant literature).

Select Characteristics of Black Men in Postsecondary Education

The characteristics of the Black male population in degree-granting institutions provide needed contextual insight into factors that can influence their success. Herein, we highlight select characteristics that have been shown by prior research to influence outcomes for Black men, with a focus on background characteristics (e.g., age, dependency, generation status) and environmental pressures. In terms of background characteristics, age has been found to be an important consideration in student success. For instance, for community college men, being younger is a significant positive predictor of persistence (Hagedorn, Maxwell, & Hampton, 2007; Perrakis, 2008) and likelihood to transfer (Wood & Palmer, in press). The average age of a Black undergraduate male in postsecondary education is 27.5. This mean age is influenced by public two-year and private for-profit enrollees who are, on average, 28 and 31 years of age. In contrast, the mean age of Black men enrolled in public four-year institutions is only 24.1 years old (see Table 5).

In general, the majority of Black men in college are independents (as opposed to being dependents). Typically, being an independent suggests that a student is not dependent upon parents/guardians to support their academic endeavors. There are numerous ways in which students can qualify as independents; they include being 24 years of age or older, married, having dependents, active duty or veteran status, ward of the court, or homeless (NPSAS, 2012c). While only 38.6% of Black males in public four-year colleges are independents, a large proportion of these men in public two-year colleges and for-profit colleges and universities are independent, 61.7% and 80.7%, respectively. This represents a large number of students in these institutional types who have the added pressure of engaging in postsecondary education without the "assumption" of support from others.

Another core background consideration is generation status. Research has shown that first-generation students are significantly less likely to succeed than those whose parents have earned a college degree (Freeman & Huggans, 2009). In particular, first-generation students typically have more limited cultural and social capital needed for success in academia in comparison to their non-first-generation peers (Strayhorn, 2006). Overall, two thirds of Black male collegians are first-generation college goers (67.7%). The percentage of first-generation students is higher in public two-year colleges (at 71.8%) and private for-profit colleges (at 75.0%). However, even 60% of those in public and private not-for-profit four-year colleges are first-generation.

Though background characteristics provide contextual insight into population nuances, environmental pressures provide more insight into collegiate success. Environmental pressures relate to factors that are outside of college that influence student success in college. These factors serve as a primary predictor of attrition among Black men in college (Wood & Williams, 2013). As noted previously, one of the characteristics associated with being an independent is marital status. The data illustrate that Black men in public four-year institutions are less likely to be married than their peers in other sectors. Specifically, only 9.8% of these men are married in comparison to 21.7% in

TABLE 5
Select Characteristics of Black Males by Institutional Type

	Average Age	Independent	Married	With Dependents	First Generation	Veteran	Average Income
Total	27.5	57.7%	15.5%	26.8%	67.7%	7.1%	$32,747
Public four-year	24.1	38.6%	9.8%	15.2%	60.9%	3.5%	$38,358
Private not-for-profit four-year	26.4	40.2%	16.6%	20.9%	60.0%	6.3%	$42,297
Public two-year	28.0	61.7%	15.8%	28.3%	71.8%	6.3%	$29,558
Private for-profit	31.0	80.7%	21.7%	42.1%	75.0%	12.9%	$25,974
Others	27.7	58.4%	15.0%	24.5%	60.3%	9.2%	$36,946

Source: National Postsecondary Student Aid Study. (2012b). *NPSAS institution sector (4 with multiple) by dependency status, marital status, parents' highest education level, veteran status, types of dependents, average age as of 12/31/2011, average adjusted gross income (AGI).* Washington, DC: U.S. Department of Education, National Center for Education Statistics.

for-profit institutions. However, an even more salient environmental factor is whether or not a student has dependents. Dependents include those who the student provides support for, and can include children, parents, grandparents, and others who are financially dependent upon the student. Black males at public four-year colleges are the least likely to have dependents (at 15.2%), while those attending public two-year colleges are nearly twice as likely (at 28.3%) to have dependents. However, these data are dwarfed by the percentage of for-profit Black men with dependents, of which 42.1% are responsible for supporting others. This level of external responsibility can place great pressure on Black men as they seek to negotiate their external responsibilities with their collegiate commitments.

In recent years, especially since the ending of the conflicts in Afghanistan and Iraq, colleges and universities have seen a rise in veteran populations. Though relatively underexplored in the scholarly literature, 7.1% of Black male collegians (across institutional types) are veterans, with the smaller percentage at public four-year colleges (3.5%) and the largest representation of veterans at for-profit institutions (12.9%). What is known is that veteran students, in general, struggle in becoming socially integrated into the campus setting, face challenges in financing college due to GI bill limitations, and may have health impairments (e.g., post-traumatic stress disorder, physical disabilities) as a result of their service (DiRamio, Ackerman, & Mitchell, 2008). While the enrollment data presented are recent (from 2012), the effect of troop withdrawals on higher education enrollment is poised to increase, as is the need to address the unique challenges of veterans who are also Black men and the myriad of associated structural and institutional inhibitors to their success (see subsequent chapters).

Financial stability is an integral component needed for collegiate success. Mason (1998) found that financial barriers are a chief inhibitor (negative predictor) of Black male success in college. Thus, it is important to consider the variation in financial average income for Black men by institutional type. The average income of a Black male collegian is $32,747 per year. However, by institutional type, two noticeable characteristics emerge. First, Black men in private not-for-profit institutions have the highest average incomes (at $42,297) while Black men in private for-profits ($25,974) have the lowest incomes, followed by those in the community college (at $29,558). While these income gaps may be explained by differences in dependency status and the age of the respondents, the impact of limited fiscal resources on collegiate success remains a concern.

Taking into account the select characteristics of Black males presented herein, several key considerations are evident. First, Black male background characteristics and environmental pressures differ significantly by institutional type, with the greatest variation seen between public four-year and for-profit institutions. Second, Black males in public four-year colleges are characterized by several interrelated factors; in comparison to their same race-gender peers in other institutional types, they tend to be younger, more dependent, single, and are less likely to be veterans and first-generation. In other words, these men (based solely on these select factors alone) may face fewer environmental barriers to academic and social inclusion than their peers in other institutional types. Third, from the opposite perspective, Black men in public two-year and for-profit colleges face greater environmental challenges than their peers, particularly those at public four-year institutions. They are more likely to be older, independent, married, have dependents, and to be first-generation. Moreover, for-profit colleges also have a greater percentage of Black men who are veterans and lower income (comparatively). These data suggest that real differences are evident across institutional types that distinguish the Black male populations, thereby suggesting a need for programs, policies, practices, and services specific to their respective needs (Wood, 2013). In all, Black men in college are not a monolithic group, but are indeed very diverse across institutional sectors (Hilton et al., 2012).

Educational Outcomes

With this context in mind, we provide some information relevant to disparate outcomes for Black men in comparison to their male peers as well as examining variation across institutional sectors. According to national data, two thirds of Black men who start college never finish (Cuyjet, 2006; Harper, 2006a; Palmer et al., 2009). Table 6 presents graduation data for full-time certificate/degree seeking undergraduate men enrolled in public four-year institutions. The graduation rates are presented at 150% of normal time (a

TABLE 6
Six-Year Graduation Rates for Full-Time Certificate/Degree Seeking Men by Cohort

	1996	2000	2001	2002	2003	2004
White	50.8	53.8	54.5	54.4	55.9	56
Black	**30.3**	**34.1**	**33.1**	**32.9**	**32.9**	**32.7**
Hispanic	37.5	41.1	41.1	41.4	42.3	43
Asian	55.2	60	60.6	61.3	62.7	62.9
American Indian	33.1	33.6	33.8	32.2	34.9	34.9
Nonresident	48.8	52.1	52.5	52.5	53.3	53

Source: Integrated Postsecondary Education Data System (IPEDS). (2014) *Fall 2001 and Spring 2002 through Spring 2011, Graduation rates component.* Washington, DC: U.S. Department of Education, National Center for Education Statistics.

six-year graduation rate) by cohort. For example, between 2004 and 2010, 32.7% of Black men enrolled in a public four-year college or university would have graduated. For this year, Black men were the lowest performing male group, with Asians, nonresidents, and Whites possessing higher graduation rates. However, across the time span presented in Table 6, it should be noted that Black males rotate with American Indian males as the group with the lowest graduation rates. For example, while Black men had the lowest graduation rates in 1996, 2001, 2003, and 2004, American Indian males had lower rates in 2000 and 2002. This is not to problematize these historically underrepresented and underserved men, but to illustrate that institutions of higher education are ineffective in serving their needs while graduating significantly higher percentages of other male groups.

Another interesting trend seen from these data is the increase in graduation rates over time. The data clearly reflect a trend of higher success rates from 1996 to 2004. Asians and Whites experienced the highest gains during this time frame, with total graduation rate increases by 7.7% and 5.2%, respectively. In contrast, Black and American Indian men experienced the lowest gains at 2.4% and 1.8%. Much of the rise in rates is a result of the increase in rates from the 1996 cohort to the 2000 cohort. Interestingly, after this period, Black men are the only group to have experienced successive decreases in graduation rates, from 34.1% in 2000 to 32.7% in 2004. While not strikingly

TABLE 7
First Degree Type Attained Through 2009 by First Institution Sector (Level and Control) 2003–2004 for Race/Ethnicity (Black or African American) and for Gender (Male)

First Degree Type Attained Through 2009	Attained	No Degree	Total
Total	35.6	64.4	100%
Public four-year	48.6	51.4	100%
Private not-for-profit four-year	49.2	50.8	100%
Public two-year	24.0	76.0	100%
Private for-profit	41.3	58.7	100%
Others	22.0	78.0	100%

Source: BPS. (2009a). *Beginning Postsecondary Students Longitudinal Study. First degree attained through 2009 by institutional sector level and control and (Black) and (male).* Washington, DC: National Center for Education Statistics.

large, this percentage decrease illustrates a differential pattern than experienced by other men. Moreover, it reifies concerns among many academics that have led to a rise in scholarship on Black males. However, despite the burgeoning literature base, institutions of higher education have remained unsuccessful in facilitating academic gains for these men.

Success rates (e.g., persistence, achievement, attainment) for Black men vary greatly by institutional type. Table 7 presents attainment rates as a guidepost for examining cross-institutional success. The data present in this table are based on the longitudinal outcomes data from the 2003–2004 Beginning Postsecondary Students Longitudinal Study (BPS, 2009a). Attainment was operationalized as part-time and full-time students who achieved a certificate, associate's degree, or bachelor's degree by 2009. At public and private not-for-profit four-year colleges, slightly less than half (48.6% and 49.2%) of Black men will obtain a degree in six years. This rate is higher than that at for-profit institutions (41.3%). At public two-year institutions, the attainment rate is much lower at 24.0%. Here, some context may be needed. Not all students enter the community college with the intent of earning a certificate or degree. Some students will intend to transfer (without earning a degree) while other students will have no degree intentions at all. For instance, in these data, 11.3% had no degree intentions (BPS, 2009b). Regardless of these

TABLE 8
Total Degrees Awarded by HBCU and All Institutions in 2009–2010

Degree Type	HBCU Total	All Institutions Total	HBCU Percent of All Institutions
Associate's	516	36,136	1.42%
Bachelor's	9,327	56,171	16.60%
Master's	1,488	22,120	6.72%
Doctoral	454	3,622	12.53%

Source: Digest of Education Statistics. (2011b). *Integrated Postsecondary Education Data System, "Fall Enrollment Survey" (IPEDS-EF:90); Spring 2001 and Spring 2011, Enrollment component; Spring 2011, Finance component; and Fall 2010, Completions component.* Washington, DC: U.S. Department of Education, National Center for Education Statistics.

considerations, the attainment outcomes for Black men in public two-year institutions are concerning.

As noted previously, HBCUs present another layer of complexity in contextualizing the effect of institutional type on Black male success. A number of scholars had extolled the importance and success of HBCUs in fostering outcomes for their students (Allen & Jewell, 2002; Berger & Milem, 2000; Brown, 1999a; Fries-Britt & Turner, 2002; Palmer & Gasman, 2008). In particular, these scholars note that HBCUs provide environments that promote belonging, affirmation, Black identity, and personal growth (Allen, 1992; Bonous-Hammarth & Boatsman, 1996; Flowers, 2002; Outcalt & Skewes-Cox, 2002). The tangible outcomes of such environments are evident in viewing data for the total degrees awarded to Black men. While HBCUs account for only 2.1% of the 4,868 degree-granting institutions, they graduate high percentages of Black men (especially at the bachelor's and doctoral levels; see Table 8). For example, in 2009–2010, of the total of 56,171 bachelor's degrees awarded to Black men, 9,327 (16.6%) were awarded to Black men attending HBCUs. Similarly, at the doctoral level, HBCU degrees to Black men accounted for 12.53% of the total doctorates awarded to Black men (Digest of Education Statistics, 2011b). Indeed, while HBCUs graduate a large number of Black men, many of these institutions are experiencing challenges to the retention and persistence of Black men. Further benefits and challenges relevant to HBCUs are discussed in the third chapter.

The aforementioned outcome data illustrate four compelling points. First, Black men in public four-year colleges and universities are generally the lowest performing male group (rotating occasionally with their American Indian peers). Thus, the enhanced focus on Black men in postsecondary education research is warranted given the dismal success of institutions in fostering positive outcomes for these men in comparison to their White, Asian, and nonresident peers. Second, cohort trend data illustrate that the challenges facing Black men may be worsening given the small decline in six-year graduation rates for these men across successive cohorts from 2000 to 2004. Third, some institutional types perform better in fostering Black male attainment than others, particularly private not-for-profit and public four-year institutions. In contrast, public two-year college attainment rates are alarmingly low. This suggests a greater need to focus on programming and interventions at these colleges that can increase their capacity to serve Black men. Fourth, HBCUs serve as a critical linchpin in fostering the success (e.g., retention, bachelor's degree attainment) of Black men. These institutions award a significantly high proportion of degrees to Black men, especially at the bachelor and doctoral degree levels.

Given the data highlighted in this chapter (e.g., enrollment trends, select student characteristics, academic outcomes) as well as the rise of research on Black men in college, it is clear that the focus of this monograph on Black men is timely, relevant, and necessary. As previously noted, this monograph provides scholars in the field with a compelling overview of the status of the field. We expect that this monograph will generate new insights and revised perspectives that illuminate new areas of research with fresh lines of questioning. Ultimately, our goal is to advance research and practice in the field of postsecondary education with the aim of better understanding the experiences, educational realities, and outcomes of Black men. This aim is critical given that many Black men vest their personal, academic, and career goals in higher education institutions, often with an unequivalent commitment in return.

Overview of the Monograph

This monograph features four chapters. Each chapter addresses a unique aspect of the findings from our literature metasynthesis. In the second chapter, *Getting to College: Factors Affecting Black Male Achievement in Schools and the Educational Pipeline*, we focus on the experiences of Black males in preK–12 education. Specifically, we emphasize research focused on the factors that foster or hinder success among those students. This chapter is critical to gaining a foundational and contextual understanding of the experiences and outcomes of Black male collegians, as many of the problems impeding students' access to and persistence through higher education emerge prior to college entry. For example, at least three reasons—lack of quality teachers, overrepresentation of Black male students in special education courses, and lack of minority peers in advanced placement courses in preK–12 education—hinder the participation and success of Blacks in higher education.

Undergirded by this context, the third chapter, *Factors Critical to the Access and Success of Black Men in Postsecondary Education*, examines the experiences of Black men in higher education. That is, we provide a broad review of the literature programs, factors, and practices that promote access and success of Black male college students in various institutional contexts. The chapter, therefore, serves to inform researchers, practitioners, and policymakers on how to implement initiatives promoting the success of Black male collegians.

The final chapter of this monograph, *Implications for Future Research, Policy, and Practice*, sets forth new directions for research and action relevant to Black men in college. Specifically, the fourth chapter includes recommendations for researchers, as well as implications for higher education policymakers, practitioners, and preK–12 professionals. We identify critical areas for future research on Black male students in preK–12 and higher education. We also make recommendations for higher education policymakers and practitioners regarding ways to implement and maintain programs and practices that will maximize access and success among Black male students.

Getting to College: Factors Affecting Black Male Achievement in Schools and the Educational Pipeline

A LARGE SEGMENT OF STUDENTS enrolled in U.S. schools fail to gain access to high-quality education despite school reform efforts, increased standardization in schools, the influx of charter schools, commitments to high-stakes testing, and increased school district oversight by states and corporations (Brown, Dancy, & Norfles, 2007; Darling-Hammond, 2006; Howard, 2010). The ways in which access trends risk U.S. global competitiveness and industry productivity are common parlance, especially following the publication of the report *A Nation at Risk: The Imperative for Educational Reform* (U.S. Department of Education, The National Commission on Excellence in Education, 1983), which required more rigorous academic standards (Henfield, Moore, & Wood, 2008; Howard, 2013; Prakash & Waks, 1985). Over 20 years later, the Organisation of Economic Cooperation and Development (OECD) found the U.S. ranked 15th in the number of students entering and completing higher education, a glaring drop from the once-held second rank position (Callan, 2006).

The acknowledgement that many nations have surpassed the United States in rates of college participation and degree attainment also requires a critical focus on the declining educational attainment of children and young adults (Callan, 2006; Palmer, Davis, Moore, & Hilton, 2010; Wagner, 2006).

Furthermore, national obsession with quantifiable assessments of mental proficiency overshadows other conceptions of educational excellence—namely, high-ordered analytical thinking, self-actualization, and social responsibility, which benefit society in sundry and immense ways (Prakash & Waks, 1985). While the "rising tide of mediocrity" noted in *A Nation at Risk* affects all students, persistent data show that certain student groups are more severely and disproportionately affected by the failures of society and its educational institutions.

It is well established in the literature that Black males remain one of the most socially and academically marginalized student groups in U.S. schools (Brown, Dancy, & Davis, 2013; Dancy & Brown, 2012; Ferguson, 2000; Howard, 2013; Lewis & Erskine, 2008; Noguera, 2008; Polite & Davis, 1999). Characterizing this marginalization are differential achievement rates and school completion; curricular inequities; overexpulsions and suspensions; overrepresentations in special, general, and vocational education; and underrepresentation in rigorous or gifted and talented courses (Garibaldi, 1992; Hrabowski, Maton & Greif, 1998; Noguera, 2001; Ross, 2012). While the plight of Black males in schools is well documented, there has been little change in policy or practice and little learning from this student group that is not associated with negative indicators (Garibaldi, 1992; Holzman, 2010; Hopkins, 1997; Price, 2000). These realities are consistent with sociohistorical, political, and economic realities of what it means to be Black boys and men in the United States.

Black males are disproportionately born into lives of challenge; they suffer disproportionately high infant mortality rates, are reared in chronic and abject poverty, and are overrepresented in underfunded schools (Anderson, 2008). The persistence of social ills in Black males reveals unique and deleterious effects even unto adulthood (Dancy, 2012; Howard, 2013). For instance, Black males experience chronically high unemployment, overincarceration, disparate health conditions, and ultimately lower life expectations than any of the largest racial/ethnic and gender groups in the United States (Howard, 2013; U.S. Department of Commerce, Census Bureau, American Community Survey, 2007–2009). Black males also occupy a paradox in the psyche of the United States which plays out in school and society; they are both admired and despised (Dancy & Brown, 2012; Davis, 1994, 2001). Pedestrian praise of Black male heroics in peer and athletic circles in schools also manages coexistence with public labels as problems, violent, scary, and hypersexual. Public enjoyment of Black male talent and genius in music and entertainment concurrently survives with modern-day police and neighborhood lynchings of unarmed Black males. In her discussion of the "U.S. love-hate relationship with Black males" (p. 8), Ladson-Billings (2011) observes,

> *We see Black males as "problems" that our society must find ways to eradicate. We regularly determine them to be the root cause of most problems in school and society. We seem to hate their dress, their language, and their effect. We hate that they challenge authority and command so much social power. While the society apparently loves them in narrow niches and specific slots—music, basketball, football, track—we seem less comfortable with them in places like the national Honor Society, the debate team, or the computer club. (p. 9)*

While awareness of the issues confronting Black males has increased, public and school failures to institutionalize supports persist. Therefore, the purpose of this chapter is threefold. First, we briefly review sociohistorical and legal contexts for understanding Black male access and achievement in the educational pipeline. The educational pipeline metaphor describes critical stages in the educational process for Black male students and points decision makers where and how to intervene (Jackson, 2007). Second, we review the current landscape of Black male experiences and outcomes in U.S. schools. The third and final section identifies explanations tied to schooling conditions, community, home, and background factors. While we pay attention to issues of identity intersectionality (Crenshaw, 1989) as appropriate to disrupt monolithic portrayals of Black males, the focus of this chapter is to elucidate the educational challenges and factors that cut across multiple identities.

The U.S. Black Educational Pipeline: Sociohistorical and Policy Perspectives

Examining the sociohistorical and policy contexts under which Blacks attained primary and secondary education reveals the struggle for educational attainment as well as a deeper understanding of what is required to promote equitable change. Furthermore, the tools of policy design require attention as they require individuals to act with the intention of solving public problems or attaining policy goals (Baker, 2001; Jackson, 2007). This section broadly defines policy tools that continue to affect Black male education and the sociohistorical matters to which these tools responded. While not a complete history, this section draws upon national policy and legal impact on schools and schooling.

Prior to the Era of Reconstruction, very few educational opportunities existed for Blacks. The Slave Codes expressly prohibited any efforts to educate enslaved men, women, and children. Indeed, endeavoring to protect both the peculiar institution and the South itself, every state except Tennessee enacted laws preventing the enslaved from being educated (Brown & Dancy, 2008). Although some enslaved and "masters" circumvented these laws, very few Blacks were literate at the time they gained their freedom (Foner, 1988; Roebuck & Murty, 1993).

Following the end of the Civil War, many recognized the need to provide educational opportunities for freed men and women. The education of Blacks remained a thoroughly debated issue even though substantial efforts (i.e., the founding of historically Black colleges) were ongoing throughout the South. The social and economic instability of the South following the Civil War helped perpetuate the fear that educating freedmen would lead to racial upheaval (Bond, 1935; Clement, 1966; Roebuck & Murty, 1993). Although they did not generally support the idea of schooling for Blacks, some Whites did recognize the social, political, and economic advantages these education efforts afforded them (Anderson, 1988; Engs, 1999; Spivey, 1978). As Donald Spivey (1978) suggests, maintaining control over Black education helped Southern Whites institute a "new slavery" during the Reconstruction Era.

The "new slavery" brought new efforts to emancipate Blacks with education as method. These efforts were hard-fought and influenced by the ideologies and debates of the day. Viewing himself as a champion of the cause of freedmen, Samuel Chapman Armstrong was instrumental in furthering the efforts of Southern Whites to control Black education. The son of Hawaiian missionaries, Armstrong served in the Union Army leading Black troops. While stationed in the Sea Islands of South Carolina, Armstrong began to recognize the similarities between the circumstances confronting the former slaves and the native Hawaiian people his parents dedicated their lives to saving. Acknowledging their eagerness to learn, Armstrong believed that freedmen needed proper training to survive in the "White world" (Engs, 1999; Hall, 1973).

In 1865, the U. S. Freedman Bureau was established by Congress to assist newly free enslaved Blacks with food, medicine, jobs, contracts, legal matters, and education. The Bureau subsequently established over 4,000 schools for Blacks. A few decades later, the *Plessy v. Ferguson* (1896) decision upheld that states have the constitutional authority to provide "separate but equal" accommodations for Blacks. One of the more significant postsecondary admission cases that forced states to establish separate professional programs for Blacks occurred in 1938, *Missouri ex rel. Gaines v. Canada* (Jackson, 2007).

The idea behind school desegregation was originally to provide better education for Black students (Halpern, 1995; Kluger, 1975). This logic posited that a desegregated education would grant Black students access to resources, networks, and opportunities currently unavailable in their segregated schools. The original logic, however, did not prescribe any alteration in the culture, climate, or constitution of the instructional setting, which already embodied equity, efficiency, community, security, and liberty. While the segregated school systems provided a uniquely affirming educational environment for Black students within the social era, the logic argued that desegregated schools would provide new intellectual outlets (Dancy & Brown, 2008). Further, the contention was that desegregated schools would be catalysts for universal social mobility.

While school desegregation in theory promoted equal opportunity in education, this concept failed to provide meaningful guidance for efficient student outcomes. Brown and Dancy (2008) argue that this consequence revealed the tensions between "equity" proponents and "efficiency" proponents. Equity proponents primarily fight to ensure equality irrespective of conflicting political and rational ideologies. Efficiency proponents, however, primarily address costs and benefits as well as inputs and outputs. This market of economic and social capital demands high levels of quality assurance, characterized by the least possible deficits and deficiencies in educational outcomes.

The existing stratagem of educational opportunity persisted until a series of cases were filed by Black students seeking admission to "historically White institutions" (Brown, 1999a). Thus, the preceding higher education integration cases served as jurisprudential planks for *Brown v. Board of Education of Topeka* (1954). The Supreme Court ruled in the *Brown v. Board of Education of Topeka* (1954) decision that school settings restricted by race were unconstitutional. As the watershed ruling regarding segregated public education, *Brown v. Board of Education of Topeka* (1954) establishes the judicial and social standard for open access within school settings. More specifically, *Brown* had two primary planks: (a) a formal rebuke and condemnation of the American system of apartheid in public education and (b) the issuance of a clarion call for the provision of educational opportunities for Black students (Carter, 1996; Lagemann & Miller, 1996; Wolters, 1984). Policymakers hailed these two planks as the remedy for all of America's social ills; they believed that 300 years of social, civic, and educational disparity could be resolved via a new initiative—school desegregation. However, despite evidence of "good faith," the formal structures of school desegregation did not eradicate the racial hierarchalization that was now wedded to the national social structure, nor the damage to the collective and individual consciousness of the citizenry (Brown, 1999a). Leon Higginbotham (1996) elaborates on this point. Higginbotham posits that the

> *Brown v. Board of Education ... decision merely struck down state-enforced segregation in public schools. It did not, however, convince a great many white parents in either the North or the South to*

send their children to school with black children ... Eventually the precept of black inferiority and white superiority worked itself into the fabric of the American legal process. The social and color ladder became a legal one as well. Looking for evidence of the precept of inferiority in the American legal process, however, is very much like looking for evidence of slavery in the United States Constitution as originally ratified ... Similarly the legal process institutionalized the premise of black inferiority without ever specifically delineating in any one case or statute the entire rationale for the precept of black inferiority ... But the legal process as a whole was more subtle in assimilating and perpetuating an ideology in which whiteness was the nimbus of superiority, and blackness the stigma of inferiority. (pp. 15–16)

The Brown ruling was first applied to higher education when the *Florida ex rel. Hawkins v. Board of Control of Florida* (1956) suit reached the Supreme Court. The case involved Virgil Hawkins and three other Black students who were denied admission to the University of Florida's law school. The ruling highlighted the potential impotence of the Brown ruling in relation to American education. In fact, in order "to free itself from the constraints of the Brown implementation decree, they [National Association for the Advancement of Colored People] cited the whole roster of pre-Brown higher education cases to support Hawkins's claim for immediate relief" (Preer, 1982, p. 141). Hawkins was never admitted to the University of Florida's law school, and many speculated that "had it not been for the advent of Brown ... Hawkins would have been decided differently" (Jenkins, 1958, p. 200). Beyond the myriad faults, flaws, and failures of the school desegregation cases, the general criticism remains: legal precedent is ineffectual in resolving the issue of Black student achievement in the P–16 pipeline, much less the prevailing psychological shackles of racial inferiority on America's public logic (Brown, 1999b; Stefkovich & Leas, 1994). The trend data and research in the following section define how battles for educational access play out in the contemporary lives of Black males.

Black Males in U.S. Schools: A National Framework

Today, the majority of babies born in the United States are babies of color (U.S. Census Bureau, 2011). As communities reflect this trend, U.S. democracy and the labor market must respond to changing realities. Even more, academic outcomes in K–12 education are critical components to higher education enrollment, completion, and lifelong career success. Thus, schools and colleges must engage mutually constitutive issues connected to social, civic, and economic prosperity. While a high school diploma was the primary pathway to individual and collective opportunity in America, the high school diploma today is critical for entry into postsecondary training (Schott Foundation for Public Education, 2012). The data on Black male participation and educational attainment are bleak and suggest deficits in the structures, policies, practices, and programs purported to serve them.

Black males comprise close to four million, or 7% of the U.S. student population (Snyder & Dillow, 2012). Data in *The Urgency of Now: The Schott 50 State Report on Public Education and Black Males* (Schott Foundation for Public Education, 2012) noted that Black males are the least likely to secure a regular diploma four years after beginning high school. The report also included an analysis of state-reported graduation rate data (2009–2010) and found that, in 38 of the 50 states and the District of Columbia, Black males have the lowest graduation rates among Black, Latino, and White male and female students. It should be noted that Latino males had the lowest graduation rates in the other 11 states.

In general, only 52% of Black males graduate from high school in four years while 78% of White males graduate in four years. Yet the national graduation rate for Black males has increased by 10 percentage points, from 42% in 2001–2002 to 52% in 2009–2010 (Schott Foundation for Public Education, 2012). However, the progress over nine years toward closure of the Black male and White male graduation gap has only achieved a three-percentage point gain, from a 29 percentage point gap to 26. According to the Schott Foundation Report, it would take nearly 50 years for Black males to secure the same high school graduation rates as their White male peers. Therefore, the urgency is not only about educational attainment but also the speed with which education reform efforts meet the disparate rate of graduation. Sadly, breakdowns of data at the state level tell a disturbing story.

Black male graduation rates in New York are among the lowest in the nation. A meager 37% of Black boys graduate from New York high schools in four years in comparison to 78% of their White male counterparts. Additional states with glaringly large gaps between graduation rates for Black and White males include the District of Columbia (50%), Iowa (49%), and Nebraska (43%). States with relatively small Black populations achieve high graduation rates for Black male students and suggest that Black males, on average, perform better when they are not relegated to underresourced districts or schools. When provided similar opportunities, Black males produce similar or better outcomes as their White male peers (e.g., Maine, Utah, Vermont, Idaho; Schott Foundation for Public Education, 2012). On average, states with low graduation rates for Black male students (e.g., New York, Nebraska, South Carolina) tend to have concentrations of those students in underresourced districts where both Black and White male students perform poorly. However, two key interventions are identified in school districts with the highest graduation rates for Black males. First, on average, states and districts that limit the impact of poverty and resource disparities on students reach better outcomes. Second is the role of innovative support-based programming as a valuable intervention in school districts. While school districts in New York reform education based on standards, the district has not provided supports for a critical mass of Black males to reach the standards (Schott Foundation for Public Education, 2012). One related area requiring intervention is the issue of temporary school closings, or "snow days," which correlate with the achievement of Black students in disparate ways (Schott Foundation for Public Education, 2012).

The Schott Foundation Report (Schott Foundation for Public Education, 2012) also argues that Black males are at the center of a "pushout crisis" and identifies two ways in which Black students, particularly males, are kept out of schools. First, the report noted that third graders who attend schools with an average of five unscheduled closures report reading and math achievement scores that are nearly 3% lower than third graders who attend schools with no closings. Fewer learning opportunities as well as other factors contributing to school absence only exacerbate achievement gaps for Black students. For instance, chronic absenteeism is linked to lower achievement while more time devoted to learning is highly correlated with higher achievement (Dobbie & Fryar, 2011). A second and more well-established issue in the literature is the glaring suspension of Black males (Brown et al., 2013; Dancy & Brown, 2012; Howard, 2013; Losen & Gillespie, 2012).

A report from Losen and Gillespie (2012), affiliated with the Center for Civil Rights Remedies at UCLA's Civil Rights Project, indicates that over three million students were suspended at least one time in the 2009–2010 academic year. Students who have been suspended are three times more likely to drop out of school by the 10th grade when compared to students who have never been suspended. Furthermore, students who drop out of school are three times more likely to be incarcerated in their lives (Schott Foundation for Public Education, 2012). When these students return to school, they are sanctioned in inequitable ways including increased barriers to guidance counselors, mentors, or mental health professionals who could support their needs. Black males are three times more likely than White, Latino, and Asian males to be suspended from elementary and secondary schools (Aud, Fox, & Kewal Ramani, 2010; Losen & Gillespie, 2012). Not only are the wages of suspension associated with sociocognitive development but also learning and retention.

Administrative discipline policies are largely correlated with decreased learning outcomes and increased student attrition (Schott Foundation for Public Education, 2012). In the United States, nearly one out of every six Black students (17%) was suspended at least once in 2009–2010, compared to one in 20 White students (95%). More extreme cases include a school district in Pontiac, Michigan in which 66% of Black students have been suspended at least once (Schott Foundation for Public Education, 2012). While the "pushout crisis" is troubling, the Schott Foundation Report (Schott Foundation for Public Education, 2012) also calls attention to America's "lockout crisis" as a simultaneous phenomenon. This crisis describes the pathological blocking of Black male access to several critical resources that support learning.

As the country moves toward common core educational standards, National Association of Educational Progress (NAEP) data question whether the required supports to meet academic standards are available at state and local levels, particularly for Black males. In 2011, only 10% of Black males in the United States were proficient in Grade 8 reading as compared to 35% of White males. In fact, no state has NAEP Grade 8 reading proficiency levels for Black males above Connecticut's 19%. In addition, Black male math proficiency scores continue to significantly trail behind those of White, Latino, and Asian male counterparts despite progress over the last decade (National Center for Education Statistics, 2009). In 2009, Black males in Grades 4–8 who were not eligible for free or reduced lunch had lower math scores than White males who were eligible to receive free and reduced lunch (National Center of Educational Statistics, 2009). Black males are also most likely to be retained during their K–8 education (Howard, 2013).

The approaching national shift to a common core will likely widen gaps in performance outcomes and graduation rates (Schott Foundation for Public Education, 2012). According to the Schott Foundation 50 State Report (Schott Foundation for Public Education, 2012), West Virginia, Louisiana, California, Mississippi, Michigan, and Tennessee may be particularly vulnerable as these states are found to essentially deny educational services critical for national and global competitiveness. The Schott Report identifies five areas in which Black male achievement is hindered and/or Black male bodies are "locked out": (a) early childhood education, (b) student-centered learning, (c) well-resourced community schools, (d) gifted/talented and advanced placement opportunities, and (e) postsecondary attainment opportunities. These areas are briefly elucidated below.

Black boys are more likely than other student groups to be classified as mentally deficient or to be identified as suffering from a learning disability and placed in special education (Levin, Belfield, Muennig, & Rouse, 2007; Losen & Orfield, 2002; Moore, Henfield, & Owens, 2008; Noguera, 2012). Even though Black students account for less than 20% of the overall public school population, they are grossly overrepresented in all special education categories, accounting for 33% of students classified as mentally retarded (MR), 27% of students classified as emotionally disturbed (ED), and 18% of students classified as students labeled disabled (SLD; National Center for Education Statistics, 2007). In addition, several researchers discover teacher misunderstanding of Black male students, which severely impacts the process of overidentification for special education referrals and the underachievement of students (Howard, 2001; Neal, McCray, Webb-Johnson, & Bridgest, 2003). In fact, some Black parents and others have accused school systems across the country of using special education, a federally subsidized program tailored for children with documented disabilities, as a dumping ground for disruptive Black children (Lewis & Erskine, 2008).

A recent report from Aratani, Wight, and Cooper (2011) found socioemotional gaps in early child development among Black and White boys which only continue to grow through preschool. While this research finds significant differences between reading and mathematics achievement scores for Black and White boys in preschool, the scientists also noted that gaps in most school readiness outcomes disappear by kindergarten. Therefore, developmental gaps likely correlate with dismal realities for many Black males including low birth weight, foster care, poverty, hunger, among other challenges to this kind of development (Educational Testing Service, 2011). In addition, reading at grade level by the third grade has been identified as a benchmark with critical implications for high school completion and college transition (Schott Foundation for Public Education, 2012).

Second, student-centered learning refers to the ways in which decades of U.S. achievement gap and outcome data make clear a need for more subjective approaches that recognize Black male educational needs, social contexts, and learning styles (Schott Foundation for Public Education, 2012). It is likely that the sociocultural norms, practices, and tools that many Black males use to navigate their world are completely misaligned with their teachers (Gay & Howard, 2001; Howard, 2013). Thus, recent scholarship contends that culturally responsive educational delivery provides Black males with much better chances for school success (Brown et al., 2013; Dancy & Horsford, 2010; Howard, 2013).

Third, Black male students are prevented from the benefits associated with well-resourced community schools. At a macrolevel, the lack of adequate tax revenues in urban areas strains school funding, particularly as residents move. Furthermore, most urban districts spend at least $500 less per pupil than suburban districts (Legters, Balfanz, Jordan, & McPartland, 2004). Urban school districts serve students with greater educational needs and also face the challenges of aging facilities that require expensive maintenance and renovation. At a microlevel, property-based funding methods used to distribute existing fiscal and learning resources (e.g., access to early education and highly qualified teachers) create inherent inequities (Schott Foundation for Public Education, 2012).

Another Schott Foundation Report (Schott Foundation for Public Education, 2013), *A Rotting Apple: Education Redlining in New York City*, finds that in many urban and rural areas, inequitable resource distribution policies and practices result in "education redlining" that occurs when students' neighborhoods significantly determine performance outcomes. One of the nation's largest districts in New York City provides an example of education redlining (Schott Foundation for Public Education, 2012; Spatig-Amerikaner, 2012). The process involves segregating Black students in schools with high poverty levels, reducing critical resources for high-quality learning opportunities (including recruiting and retaining highly effective teachers) through budget and staff cuts, and subsequently leading to disproportionately high rates of teacher turnover. The result is often disproportionately closed schools or state takeovers of schools in communities of color. In this context, any chance of connecting students in these neighborhoods to well-resourced community schools is highly unlikely (Schott Foundation for Public Education, 2012).

Fourth, Black male students are noticeably underrepresented in Gifted and Talented programs in the United States and very few are allowed to take Advanced Placement (AP) classes. In New York City, few students in predominantly Black community school districts, if any, are tested for admission to Gifted and Talented programs. In other states, magnet schools are found to promote AP participation among White students but reduce participation among college-bound Black students, particularly men (Klopfenstein, 2004). These programs are traditionally better resourced, with more experienced and more highly qualified teachers (Schott Foundation for Public Education, 2012). At the high school level, Black males are generally least likely to take and pass AP courses and Black males score significantly lower than their White, Latino, and Asian counterparts in these courses (National Center for Education Statistics, 2009). Furthermore, teachers and counselors disproportionately track Black boys into low academic-ability classrooms, whereas many of their White counterparts are placed in advanced courses that prepare them for college placement in competitive institutions (Palmer & Maramba, 2011).

Fifth, a shift in the global economy toward a demand for higher order skills has placed emphasis on postsecondary education and training as a maker of opportunity in America. A recent study found that, by 2018, more than two thirds of the 47 million projected job openings will require some level of postsecondary education of training, including industry certification (Schott Foundation for Public Education, 2012). Over the last four decades, roughly 39% of American adults have held a two- or four-year degree. In many states like New York, nearly two thirds of entering college students require some remediation. In addition, financial aid supports are often not as readily available to help make this transition (Schott Foundation for Public Education, 2012). Prince and Choitz (2012) argue that the United States will need to produce about 24 million additional credentials by 2025 to keep pace with leading Organization for Economic Cooperation and Development (OECD) countries and achieve a 60% degree attainment rate among adults ages 25–64. However, at current attainment rates, the United States is on track to produce 278,500 additional credentials by 2025—a significant shortfall (Schott Foundation for Public Education, 2012). The aforementioned data in this chapter show that schooling conditions have not adequately served Black males well. Although the experiences of Black males in schools are the subject of many reports and studies, this chapter interrogates a larger body of research to inform the knowledge base more comprehensively.

W. E. B. DuBois (1903), in his groundbreaking book, *The Souls of Black Folk*, asked a rhetorical question that seems as relevant as ever today: How does it feel to be a problem? Most people in American society, including many Black Americans, view Black boys and men as problems requiring control, handling, or other forms of management (Williams, 2012). Portrayals in popular culture and media characterizations of Black men fully support the notion of Black men as problem, scary, untrustworthy, and repulsive (Dancy, 2009, 2012; Noguera, 2008; Williams, 2012). American social institutions make clear their hatred of Black males and attempts to carefully teach Black males to despise themselves (hooks, 2004a). Related to educational settings, there are several questions to engage: How, and in what ways, does this framing affect Black male behavior? What coping strategies do Black males develop? How does this influence administrator behavior and policy making in schools and collegiate settings? How do public perceptions of Black males influence teacher engagement with Black males? How are these perceptions internalized in Black male families and communities? And, finally, how do public perceptions trouble Black male academic achievement and success? The following sections explore the literature on public, community, school, home, and identity factors that challenge Black male achievement and transitions to college. While the content in this section identified what gaps exist, the following synthesis of literature takes a closer look at teacher perceptions of Black male students and teacher preparation, background, home, and community factors, and finally issues related to boyhood, masculinity, and identity.

Teacher Perceptions and Preparation

Many scholars argue that teacher perceptions and attitudes shape Black male experiences in schools; largely, they study how these perceptions have a negative effect on Black males more than any other group (Howard, 2010; Milner, 2007; Reynolds, 2010; Rios, 2011). This notion is not new to the literature. In fact, Rosenthal and Jacobson's (1968) classic study suggested that teachers' expectations may influence the academic performance of school-aged children. This practice, which the authors called the pygmalion effect, is cited as one of the reasons that many Black students, males in particular, are disengaged in schools. Rist's (1970) study further highlighted how the pygmalion effect can happen as early as kindergarten and the ways in which students internalize teachers' attitudes, affecting academic experiences, performances, and outcomes. Rong's (1996) study showed that teachers' perceptions of student social behaviors are a result of complex interactions of students' and teachers' race and gender. The results showed that female teachers perceived female students more positively regardless of teachers' race. And while White female teachers perceived White female and male students more positively than Black male students, Black female teachers made no distinction among race for students.

Hargrove and Seay (2011) studied teachers' beliefs and perceptions about low representation of Black males in gifted education. This research found different explanations between teachers of color and White teachers about the underrepresentation of Black males in gifted education. White teachers were more likely to see nonschool factors as explanations (e.g., home/parents/community) than teachers of color. White teachers also placed little attention on their instruction and beliefs as a reason for why Black males were less likely to be referred to gifted education more than any other group. Furthermore, teachers of color did not see the use of nonstandard English as a barrier to school success in the ways White teachers did. According to Howard (2013), these findings reveal deficit thinking about Black males' potential and promise in teacher perceptions.

Teachers and other school staff are also found to hold lower expectations for African American males. For instance, several researchers discovered that teachers' lower expectations of students of color, particularly males, are based on perceptions of students' current performance rather than students' potential to perform (Ferguson, 2000; Kimmel, 2000; Kober, 2001; Roderick, 2003; Trent et al., 2003). Some of this same research found Black boys to be viewed more negatively by their 9th grade teachers than Black girls (Roderick, 2003). In the classroom, many teachers operate from the frame of reference that Black males are incapable of rigor and treat them as such (Hilliard, 2000; Weiner, 2000). In addition, teachers and counselors are also far more likely to impose negative expectations upon Black males as it relates to attending college in comparison with White counterparts (Jones, 2002; Ogbu, 2003; Reid & Moore, 2008; Robinson, Stempel, & McCree, 2005). However, Black male students encouraged to view intelligence as malleable reported greater enjoyment of the academic process, greater academic engagement, and obtained higher grade point averages than their counterparts (Aronson, Fried, & Good, 2002). Not only do teacher perceptions matter, but teacher preparation is also a critical factor.

In large city schools attended by mostly Black students, many of the teachers lack proper certification for the subject areas they teach (Jordan & Cooper, 2003). Some of the most vulnerable students are often left to be taught by the least experienced individuals (Landsman & Lewis, 2006; Lewis & James, 2008; Strayhorn, 2008b; Talbert-Johnson, 2004). Cooper and Jordan (2005), for instance, found both uncertified teachers and poorly funded schools to have a negative effect on Black achievement. Teacher preparation is critical for understanding issues related to the quality of education for Black males and differences between this group and their White, and sometimes more affluent, counterparts (Hale, 2001).

Background, Family, and Community Factors

Discussed earlier in this chapter, the achievement gap begins in early childhood for Black males and actually increases as they move from grade to grade. This trend is complicated by the experience of poverty. In many cases, teenaged Black male students from poverty-ridden environments do not always have educational or reading material available in the home, which is also essential for school readiness (Alonzo, Tindal, & Robinson, 2008; Williams, Davis, Saunders, & Williams, 2002). Noguera (2001) found that many young Black males who drop out of high school do not have much support at home or at school. Conversely, Black males are more likely to graduate when there is parental support and visible models of individuals in their communities who attain education as a means of upward mobility (Toldson, Harrison, Perine, Carreiro, & Caldwell, 2006).

Parent–child interactions and parental involvement is one of the most robust predictors of Black adolescent male success in school (Howard, 2003; Toldson et al., 2006; Williams et al., 2002). When Black parents are actively involved in their sons' academic efforts by monitoring homework as well as other academic pursuits, limiting nonproductive and destructive activities (e.g., television, radio, and video games), and creating a constant and positive dialogue with the teachers and school officials, they increase the odds of their sons' success (Mandara, 2006). Toldson's (2008) research also highlights the ways Black male diet impacts academic achievement. In his work, Black male students with low academic achievement were more likely to eat junk food (potato chips, cakes, hamburgers, sweets, and cola) frequently and were less likely to regularly eat healthy food (cooked vegetables, raw vegetables, fruits, and whole wheat) compared to Hispanic and White males. This research has implications for school cafeteria menus and entails home and community interventions to regulate Black male nutrition.

The monolithic portrayal of Black males in poor urban communities fails to consider the increasing social class diversity among Black males (Howard, 2013). Gordon (2012) asserts that today approximately one third of Black families live in suburban communities and send their children to middle-class schools where they still underperform compared with their White peers. Thus, any privileges that accompany social and economic mobility do not erase the presence of race and racism when it comes to the schooling experiences of Black males. Nevertheless, researchers found families to lay the groundwork for success long before Black males get to college (Herndon & Hirt, 2004; Joe & Davis, 2010). Reynolds (2010) examined the role that parenting played in school outcomes for Black males. Her research on Black middle-class parents about their experiences in public secondary schools found Black parents' beliefs that school officials frequently excluded them from access to information that could aid them and their students. Parents also discussed the ways in which their sons were victims of lowered expectations, deficit thinking, and subject to racial microaggressions by teachers and school administrators. Notwithstanding, community-based and other success factors are also critical.

Success Factors and Resistance to Structural Inequities

One area of community intervention is the creation of single-sex schools and classrooms for Black males. Fergus and Noguera (2010) found a number of instructional strategies in single-sex schools to have a positive influence on educational experiences and outcomes for Black males. Conducted over a three-year period, their study found seven single-sex schools anchored in social/emotional programming, rites of passage programs, community service requirements, culturally responsive instruction, rigorous curriculum, and an emphasis on basic skills. The researchers additionally discovered two theories of change that guided their work: understanding the social and emotional needs of Black and Latino boys and understanding the core of their needs and targeting interventions appropriately.

Baldridge, Hill, and Davis (2011) explored the role of community-based organizations in the academic and personal development of Black males. This research centered on young Black male accounts of merely tolerating school as opposed to immersing themselves in it. Additionally identified were teachers perceived as noncaring and a number of obstacles that study participants noted led to reasonable decisions to drop out rather than remain in spaces that disaffirmed their identities and ignored their realities. However, their involvement with a community-based organization assisted the boys' transition into adulthood through positive teacher–student relationships, culturally responsive pedagogy, and the educational delivery of skills that their previous schools did not teach.

Fashola (2003) investigated the influence of after-school programs on Black male learning. The author also discovered effective programming for targeted groups of Black males and that these programs provided ongoing professional development to staff and faculty working with Black males. Specifically, Fashola identified the Boys and Girls Club and Big Brothers/Big Sisters programs, among others, as providers of support where academic deficiencies existed in Black male school experiences. Both Baldridge et al. (2011) and Fashola (2003) underscore the salient role that nonschool yet ameliorative spaces can provide for Black males. As Howard (2013) notes, these spaces have certain advantages that schools may not have including fewer restrictions on assessment measures and hiring staff, thus potentially shaping a more fruitful environment for Black males to learn.

Environments conducive to learning are also the focus of teaching interventions. Murrel (1999) found that math teachers who were responsive to social context also constructed meaningful relationships with students and had a familiarity with student discourse and modes of expression. The author additionally found that students valued question posing and teacher engagement, an eagerness to display their knowledge, and a predilection for detailed explanations.

Finally, Howard (2013) argues that the research discourse on Black males is largely absent on the supportive roles that Black males play as older siblings, part-time workers, and caregivers, and the overall tenacity and discipline they demonstrate within the home. The author further notes that dialogue about Black males often eschews recognition of discipline, commitments, and cognitive abilities even in narrow slots where Black males are often overrepresented like sports. Howard (2013) suggests that additional investigation on Black male abilities in home and out-of-class environments may also inform what is known about their learning and experiences in-class. While Black males have always demonstrated resilience and ability to be sure, this does not relieve systems and systems of their responsibility in the dismantling of inequity.

Boyhood, Masculinity, and Identity Factors

The behaviors of Black boys are salient for understanding school (mis)comprehension of masculine identities. Previous studies argued that young boys construct masculine identities and ideologies through overcoming obstacles and subsequently earning a sense of autonomy and mastery (Chodorow, 1978; Wainrib, 1992). However, scholars frame the understudied pathways of Black boys as eclectic representations of a combination of Afrocentric, Eurocentric, and alternative standards (Dancy, 2012; Harris, 1995). While Black boyhood constructions are less clear, many stereotypical ways of knowing this group abound.

Scholars found that common stereotypes including "popular youth" and "classroom terror" lead to a range of behaviors, strategies, and constructions within and beyond schooling spaces that influence how Black boys make meaning of themselves over time (Billson, 1996; Davis, 2000; Ferguson, 2000, 2007; Majors & Billson, 1992; Sewell, 1997). Black men who have attended school in American educational systems tell graphic stories that bear out this argument (Cose, 2003; Wright, 1945/2005). Their autobiographical sketches reveal the impact of disparate schooling and collegiate experiences on the construction of early manhood. In *The Envy of the World: On Being a Black Man in America*, Cose (2003) writes that poor Black children during Richard Wright's time were classified as unable to learn. In fact, Wright (1945/2005) argues that learning to read and write in his early childhood angered White American communities who wanted him to remain uneducated.

Some schooling experiences are so transformative in the lives of Black boys that they can even reverse home-grown values (Steinberg, Dornbusch, & Brown, 1992). Years ago, scholars contended that Black boys learn to behave in accordance with a culture in which "coolness" is most respected and attained by breaking rules or receiving poor grades in school (Kunjufu, 1986). Outcomes usually include social rewards like security in peer groups, achievement, belonging, status, and self-validation (Harris, 1995; Taylor, 1989). Conversely, Black males who perform well academically and/or exhibit different instincts are potentially labeled by same-race peers as "selling out" and "acting White" (Fordham & Ogbu, 1986). The likelihood of peer group acceptance or rejection, however, is not the only force that shapes masculine construction (Kunjufu, 1986; Steinberg et al., 1992).

In fact, Noguera (2001) adds that there is an institutional dynamic at play. He writes, "[Black] males may engage in behaviors that contribute to their underachievement and marginality, but are more likely to be channeled into marginal roles and to be discouraged from challenging themselves by adults who are supposed to help them" (p. 452). Ferguson (2000) makes a similar argument, asserting that Black males display aggressive behavior because they are labeled as "unsalvageable" at the beginning of their educational experiences. In *Bad Boys: Public Schools in the Making of Black Masculinity*, Ferguson (2000) found evidence that school environment contributes to the marginalization of Black boys. Specifically, labels such as "troublemakers" imposed by authorities (teachers, principals, staff members) predispose Black boys to socially unaccepted and deviant life outcomes. Additionally, Ferguson found that Black boys in the study become less eager to persist in their fourth grade year and learn to model themselves after future professional athletes or Black men in urban neighborhoods at the same time. Unfortunately, this plan is shaped for them by contexts that have labeled them as unsalvageable.

Garibaldi (1992) argues that teachers play a seminal role in reversing "unsalvageable" perceptions as well as harmful academic and social behaviors of Black boys. However, he contends that teachers are susceptible to internalizing and projecting negative stereotypes and myths to unfairly describe Black boys as a "monolithic group with little hope of survival and success" (p. 8). Garibaldi ultimately maintains that teacher locus may resist positive self-concepts and personal expectations among Black boys leading to disassociation with the learning experience.

The dominating and pervasive images of Black men as endangered species and criminals work to deny Black boys the childhood humanity they embody. Scholars refer to this illogical reality as the adultification of Black boys (Dancy, in press; Ferguson, 2000; Kunjufu, 1986). In school contexts, educators read acts of childhood transgressions as sinister, willful attitude that is stripped of any of the innocence and naivete we generally perceive in children. Ferguson's (2000) research found elementary school teachers with a tendency to invoke such images of "looters" in the Los Angeles riots of the 1990s and "refugees" in Hurricane Katrina whenever Black males did children's behavior such as borrowing library books and not returning them or returning them late. In the case of Black children, Ferguson further noted that interpretations of careless behavior are displaced by images of adult acts of theft that conjure up violence and mayhem. Thus, the assumption is that Black male children embody a malevolent, destructive, and irrational disregard for property rather than simple carelessness. What is read as natural naughtiness in White children becomes inherent viciousness and insubordination that must be controlled in Black male children. Though our culture sees children humanely and worthy of the perception of innocence, albeit immature, systems of oppression deny Black males even that benefit of the doubt.

Ferguson (2000) notes three key behaviors that emerge from biased educational systems and provide evidence that Black boys largely perceive manhood as a power struggle. The first, heterosexual power (understood as male heterosexual), refers to the physical, biological, and representational differences to perform acts (i.e., physical touching) that define Black boys as perpetrators and Black girls as victims. Personal violations of heterosexual power include transgressive behaviors (i.e., same-sex curiosity and attraction). When Black boys want to show supreme contempt for another boy they call him a girl or liken his behavior to a girl's behavior (Ferguson, 2000). In general, transgressing rigidly heterosexual masculine codes likely results in victimization and alienation from Black boy cultures at school (Davis, 2000).

A second behavior involves usage of "confrontational voice" or classroom performances that engage and disrupt the normal direction of the flow of power. While Black boys use power to disrupt the standards and well-scripted roles in classrooms (i.e., constant noise, rapping, laughing, crumpling paper), schools characterize these actions as disruption (Ferguson, 2007). Furthermore, Black boy peer groups perceive them as lively, fun, exciting, and "cool" in an otherwise bland context (Davis, 1999). However, when Black males use confrontational voices in schools, the goal is likely to make a name for themselves (Ferguson, 2007). Harper (1996) adds that how Black boys use their voice becomes an identifying marker for masculinity and that "a too-evident facility in White idiom can quickly identify one as a White-identified Uncle Tom who must also be weak, effeminate, and probably a fag" (p. 11).

Black males potentially use the third behavior, fighting, as a mechanism to demonstrate mistrust of authority figures in school due to sociohistorical and present power relations in their communities (Ferguson, 2007). Ferguson's work further contends that fighting is usually either an exploratory site to construct media-endorsed manhood, a social practice of entertainment, or an attempt to scare others to avoid future confrontations. Black boys who show competence in fighting, participating in sports, teasing, and reporting actual or contrived sexual conquests are bestowed with greater privileges than those perceived as less adequate in these areas. Corbin and Pruitt (1999) write that Black boys turn to sexual promiscuity, machismo, risk taking, and aggressive social skills to compensate for feelings of insecurity in a Eurocentric world. Such insecurity likely manifests itself in changes in posture, clothing, dialect and language, walking style, and demeanor (Harris, 1995). Majors and Billson (1992) further characterize this behavior as a coping mechanism labeled "cool pose." The authors define cool pose as

> The presentation of self that many [Black boys and] men use to establish their male identity. Cool pose is a ritualized form of masculinity that entails behaviors, scripts, physical posturing, expression management, and carefully crafted performances that deliver a single, critical message: pride, strength and control. (p. 4)

Majors and Billson (1992) argue that Black boys, prior to college, learn early to project a façade of emotionlessness, fearlessness, and aloofness to counter the poor self-image and confidence expected from the race to which they belong. Majors and Billson also suggest that the "cool pose" becomes pathological in a sense, or self-sustaining, because of its continued use as coping mechanism. To view Black boys (and men) in only this light, however, is problematic. Scholars and activists write that the endorsement of a behaviorally restrictive or unidimensional conception of manhood (i.e., tough guy, player of women) is viewed as dysfunctional in a cultural frame of racism and economic oppression (Hunter & Davis, 1992). Unfortunately, families either intentionally or unintentionally reinforce notions of unidimensional boyhood.

Black boys may also consider academic engagement less masculine because of how it is valued in families. In fact, hooks (2004b) argues that "soul-murdering" in families detrimentally affects the self-esteem of Black boys and potentially shames their authentic selves:

> In some [Black] families where reading is encouraged in girl children, a boy who likes to read is perceived as suspect, as on the road to being a "sissy". Certainly as long as [Black] people buy into the notion of patriarchal manhood, which says that real men are all body and no mind, [Black boys] who are cerebral, who want to read, and who love books will risk being ridiculed as not manly. (p. 40)

hooks reflects on experiences in her home in which her brother was constantly humiliated by her father for "not measuring up to the standards of patriarchal maleness" (p. 89). Her suggestion that Black boys are valued and indulged for being male, but also shamed for not conforming to acceptable "patriarchal boyhood" charges educational systems with failing to impart the love of learning in Black boys (p. 89). Both conditions infect the masculine identities of Black boys with powerlessness and hopelessness (hooks, 2004b).

Claude Steele (1992) has also suggested that race plays role in the educational experiences of African American boys. He argues that racial stigma is a largely ignored or unrecognized factor in the underachievement of students of color. Elaborating, he writes

Doing well in school requires a belief that school achievement can be a promising basis of self-esteem and that belief needs constant reaffirmation even for advantaged students. Tragically, I believe the lives of Black Americans are still haunted by a specter that threatens this belief and the identification that derives from it at every level of schooling. (p. 72)

Steele (1992) defines stereotype threat as anxiety or concern individuals experience in a situation in which they may confirm a negative stereotype about their social group. Steele's work has inspired examinations of the concept in the educational experiences of Black boys. For instance, Osborne (1997) found that as Black males move through high school, the correlation between academic performance and measures of their self-esteem consistently and radically declined in comparison with other groups. His findings suggest that Black males believe their fate is decided and that failure is inevitable.

Because of these early socialization experiences, researchers claim that Black boys quickly understand the social rewards associated with exhibiting masculine behaviors and derogatory name calling and peer disapproval frequently associated with feminine behaviors (Dancy, 2012; Davis, 2001; Ferguson, 2007). These experiences subsequently inform Black men's collegiate perceptions. In fact, there are a number of well-rehearsed gender roles that negatively correlate with Black men's collegiate perceptions by the time they reach traditional college age (Dancy, 2012; Fleming, 1984; Polite & Davis, 1999).

Conclusion

Public reactions to trends and outcomes in this chapter often indict Black males as creators of their problems as opposed to the incapacities of schools (Howard, 2013; Schott Foundation for Public Education, 2012). However, these reactions tend to reflect the narrow-minded and hidebound tenets of racism. Racism refers to the global system of oppression that disempowers people based on skin color and/or assumptions that people of particular races hold undesirable qualities (Omi & Winant, 1989). The extant research on Black male experiences and the educational pipeline requires common thought and consideration among all educational personnel—in schools, colleges, and other settings—who care about the educational experiences of Black males.

Many strategies (more deeply discussed in the final chapter) capture the attention of school administrators, local communities, and parents as possible solutions to the problems associated with Black males in public schools. First, mentoring programs that assign professional Black men as role models for young boys, typically in elementary and middle schools, have been established in many school districts, both urban and suburban. Second, teachers play a critical role in reversing Black boys' academic and social behaviors that conflict with educational achievement. Teachers are leaders of the classroom experience. The messages teachers consciously or subconsciously give to Black males will manifest themselves in Black males' perceptions of schools and American society. Counselors must also refrain from stereotypical thinking about the intellectual capacity and aptitude of Black males. Additionally, there are a number of implications for postsecondary educational settings.

This research joins with previous research that encourages educational institutions to mine the sources for improving context and climate. School efforts to deconstruct oppressive environments are salient for Black male achievement, retention, and the elimination of stereotypes. Stereotypes attempting to "authentically" locate Black male identities have no place in school settings and only fuel divisiveness among its stakeholders. Black boys, too, deserve equal opportunity, as any student group, to feel entitled to institutional resources deemed "good institutional practice." The delivery of these resources should not reflect a colonized institutional axiology of intolerance, closedness, and presumptuousness.

Finally, "what works" best for students in general is in many ways incompatible with "what works" for many Black males. It may be a burden for education workers to add to and constantly rethink how they deliver education to Black males. However, the implications in this chapter are likely relevant across student groups. A turbulent history of exclusion, a changing national populace, and federal policy landscape demand change and accountability.

Factors Critical to the Access and Success of Black Men in Postsecondary Education

A S INDICATED IN THE FIRST CHAPTER, increasing access to post-secondary education for Black men remains a top priority. In the second chapter, we identified factors, such as weak college preparatory curriculums, lack of quality teachers, and inadequate school funding, that hinder Black students' access to higher education. As indicated in the first and second chapters, another factor that affects access to higher education for Black students is racial discrimination (Jackson, 2007). Evidence indicates that institutional or systemic racism is embedded in many public policies, which negatively affect the educational outcomes of Black students (Harper, Patton, & Wooden, 2009).

Some of the institutional structures within schools that impede college access for Black students are nationally consistent. For example, it is well known that Black students typically do not perform well on standardized tests when compared to their White counterparts (Darling-Hammond, 2005). Steele (1997) concluded that the discrepancy in standardized test scores between Black and White students might be caused by stereotype threat, which is anxiety that arises when individuals are placed at risk of affirming a negative stereotype about their identity group. Despite the differences in test performance between Black and White students, colleges and universities continually employ such measures to determine college admission even though research suggests that standardized tests are weak measures of academic success for minority students (Hoffman & Lowitzki, 2005). While the impact of the issues discussed in the second chapter cripples the opportunity of Black students to enroll in higher education, in the subsequent section of this chapter, we discuss three programmatic initiatives—(a) TRIO programs, (b) affirmative action, and (c) college readiness programs (remedial education)—implemented to help increase access to higher education for Black students.

TRIO Programs: Facilitating Access to Higher Education for Black Students by Increasing College Readiness

TRIO programs were implemented by Congress in the 1960s to help low-income students access and succeed in higher education (Coles, 1998). Originally composed of three programs, today TRIO includes: (a) Student Support Services, (b) Educational Opportunity Centers, (c) Veteran Upward Bound, (d) Upward Bound Math-Science, and (e) the Ronald E. McNair Post Baccalaureate Achievement programs. TRIO programs are funded under Title IV of the Higher Education Act of 1965 and address the social, economic, academic, and cultural factors that make transition into higher education difficult for students who are first-generation college students. In 1999, TRIO served over 780,000 students, including 36% Black students, 16% Latino students, 5% Asian American students, 4% Native American students, and 2% students with disabilities. Collectively, TRIO provides a range of college access and support services to students throughout the educational pipeline, beginning as early as the sixth grade (Coles, 1998). These services include college readiness workshops, college academic instruction, counseling, mentorship, tutoring, and financial aid awareness seminars, all of which have been vital in helping to increase college access and success for many low-income minority students (Swail, Redd, & Perna, 2003).

Research indicates that precollege programs, such as TRIO, have been instrumental in helping to promote college access and success for low-income minority students (Coles, 1998; Harper & Kuykendall, 2012; Strayhorn, 2008c, 2013a; Swail et al., 2003; Thomas, Farrow, & Martinez, 1998). For example, Thomas et al. (1998) investigated the impact of a TRIO program on the graduation rates of the program's participants. They found that students who entered college as a result of this program were equally likely to graduate than students admitted to the university through traditional means.

While research has discussed ways in which TRIO programs promote college access and success for Black students, little research has focused specifically on Black men. Nevertheless, given the precollege experiences of many Black men described in the second chapter, we would surmise that TRIO programs have acted as a critical linchpin in helping to facilitate college access and success for Black males. Despite the efficacy of TRIO programs, they have sustained budget cuts over the years (Burd, 2011). Some have even suggested that these cuts could be exasperated by the sequester (Bidwell, 2013), which will greatly reduce the scope and impact of TRIO programs.

Affirmative Action: A Critical Facilitator of Access to Higher Education for Black Students

Since the election of the nation's first Black president, Barack Obama, some have suggested that we live in a postracial society and that programs, policies, and initiatives meant to redress systemic racism and oppression in America are no longer necessary (Lum, 2009). One such program is affirmative action. Originating with President Lyndon B. Johnson and implemented by President John F. Kennedy, affirmative action sought to promote underrepresented minorities' access and women's equity in programs using federal funds (Brown, 1999b; Froomkin, 1998). More specifically, affirmative action gave special consideration for employment, education, and contracting decisions to underrepresented minorities and women (Froomkin, 1998). Postsecondary educational institutions have generally used affirmative action to increase access among minorities and women in higher education (Kaplin & Lee, 2007).

Since its implementation, the constitutionality of affirmative action has been challenged vigorously in postsecondary education. In *University of California Regents v. Bakke* (1978), the Supreme Court ruled in a 5-to-4 vote that institutions could use race as one factor to foster diversity, but prohibited the use of racial quotas. While Bakke provided context for how other colleges and universities should tailor their affirmative action programs, the Fifth

U.S. Circuit Court of Appeals overturned Bakke, ruling that race could not be taken into account in admissions decisions (Lowe, 1999). Similarly, states, including California, Washington, Nebraska, Florida, and Arizona, have prohibited the use of affirmative action (Jaschik, 2011). Moreover, similar efforts are underway in Colorado, Missouri, and Oklahoma. Although many states have abolished affirmative action, in *Grutter v. Bollinger* (2003), the Court reaffirmed colleges and universities' ability to use race as a factor to attain a diverse student body as long as it is narrowly tailored and does not function as a quota system. Notwithstanding the Court's decision, challenges to affirmative action continue to persist. In fact, more recently, in *Fisher v. University of Texas* (2013), while the Court reaffirmed the ability of institutions to use race to diversify their student bodies, some fear that the Court's decision could lay the groundwork for future challenges and the ultimate demise of affirmative action (Barnes, 2013; Carr, 2013).

While researchers agree that the downfall of affirmation action could restrict minority students' access to predominantly White institutions (PWIs; Horn & Flores, 2003; Swail et al., 2003; Tienda, Niu, & Cortes, 2006), Harper and Griffin (2011) contend that the prohibition of affirmative action may have minimal impact on the ability of high-achieving Black men to access highly selective colleges and universities. Specifically, they interviewed 42 low-income, high-achieving students and found that they were not beneficiaries of affirmative action despite the perception by their White peers that they were. Notwithstanding Harper and Griffin's findings, for many Black men, the abandonment of affirmative action may pose a significant challenge to their ability to access a range of postsecondary educational institutions (DeSousa, 2001). However, researchers argue that the end of affirmative action may cause more Black students to attend minority-serving institutions, including HBCUs (Asquith, 2007; Palmer, 2010; Swail et al., 2003).

College Readiness Programs: A Vital Linkage to Access and Success for Black Students

In addition to affirmative action, college readiness programs (otherwise known as remedial programs) have played a critical role in increasing access and preparedness for minority students in higher education (Attewell, Lavin, Domina, & Levey, 2006; Bahr, 2008; Boylan, Bonham, & Tafari, 2005; Davis & Palmer, 2010; Kimbrough & Harper, 2006; Palmer & Davis, 2012). College remediation (sometimes referred to as developmental education) involves colleges and universities admitting students who they believe have the ability to complete a degree with some developmental assistance. Programs of this nature are designed to enhance academic deficiencies among America's underprepared college students through academic support, with program components ranging from a single course offering to more comprehensive academic and social support services, such as tutorial support, counseling, and study skill seminars (Boylan & Bonham, 2007). While research suggests that a number of undergraduates enroll in remedial courses at four-year colleges (Attewell et al., 2006; Strong American Schools, 2008), Greene and Foster (2003) found that 80% of Black students leave high school "minimally" prepared. To this end, Black students are most likely to rely on postsecondary remediation as a means for gaining access to higher education (Attewell et al., 2006).

College remediation policy is often enacted by states or state higher education systems and implemented by institutions. Despite the important role states play in determining remediation policy, state legislators appear to be unclear about what remedial education is, whom it serves, how much it costs, and who should provide it (Davis & Palmer, 2010; Merisotis & Phipps, 2000). A national survey on whether colleges and universities should give remedial education more attention revealed that 32% of legislators were in agreement, 34% were in disagreement, and 32% remained neutral (Breneman & Merisotis, 2002). States and higher education systems are raising policy questions that threaten to reduce, eliminate, or shift the costs of remediation to other systems or individuals, including the students (Bettinger & Long, 2007). These threats have been most pronounced at public four-year colleges (Parker, 2007). Because of these issues, Parker noted that roughly 22 state higher education systems have either reduced or eliminated remediation. Kimbrough and Harper (2006) noted that the elimination of college remediation has restricted access to higher education for many Black men. Specifically, they stated:

In spite of the demonstrated success of remedial programs, many state systems, including those with HBCUs have restricted access to four-year institutions by students who need to enroll in remedial programs. This policy shift has had negative effects on [Black] men . . . who previously relied upon developmental studies programs as a one chance opportunity for admission to postsecondary institutions. (p. 192)

Palmer and Davis (2012) voiced a similar concern about how the elimination of remedial programs would affect the ability of Black men to access higher education. As a result of this concern, researchers have advocated for preK–12 and postsecondary educational institutions to form alliances to help increase college preparedness among underrepresented minority students in general and Black men specifically (Davis & Palmer, 2010; Kimbrough & Harper, 2006; Merisotis & Phipps, 2000; Palmer & Davis, 2012).

In sum, research has identified TRIO programs, affirmative action, and college readiness programs as serving as important gateways to higher education for Black students. While the precollege experience of many Black males necessitate their participation in these programs to access postsecondary education, as budgets are increasingly cut for these programs and others are phrased out via court or policy initiatives, Black males may face a harder time accessing higher education.

Black Men at Historically Black Colleges and Universities

Despite the fact that fewer Black students are attending HBCUs (Palmer & Maramba, in press; Sissoko & Shiau, 2005), due largely to the promulgation of governmental initiatives and litigation designed to integrate the education of Blacks and Whites, these institutions continue to play a prominent role in serving as a linchpin for Black students to access higher education (Fries-Britt & Turner, 2002; Kim & Conrad, 2006; Palmer & Gasman, 2008). HBCUs are known for providing a supportive and family-like environment that helps to facilitate students' self-efficacy, racial pride, psychological wellness, academic development, and persistence (Fries-Britt & Turner, 2002; Kim & Conrad, 2006; Palmer & Gasman, 2008). Black students at HBCUs reportedly have stronger academic self-concepts, are more satisfied with their college experience, and are engaged at higher levels than their same race counterparts at PWIs (Fleming, 1984; Fries-Britt & Turner, 2002; Harper & Gasman, 2008).

Research from other scholars has supported the impact that HBCUs have on the retention and persistence of Black students (e.g., Gasman, 2008; Gasman, Lundy-Wagner, Ransom, & Bowman, 2010; Ross, 1998). Kim and Conrad (2006) pointed out that one of the factors that make HBCUs unique is their ability to achieve these outcomes while lacking funding parity with their PWI counterparts. While research overwhelmingly supports the impact that HBCUs have on Black students, some research has noted that a number of HBCUs have high attrition rates because they enroll a high number of first-generation, low-income, Pell-eligible students (Gasman, 2013). Furthermore, other threads of research on HBCUs have commented on the gender imbalances on many of these campuses (Gasman, 2013). Gasman noted that there are five HBCUs that have more men than women enrolled (i.e., Arkansas Baptist College, Edward Waters College, Concordia College-Selma, Livingstone College, and Texas College); however, on the majority of HBCU campuses, the opposite is true.

Not only are more women enrolling in HBCUs, they are also more likely than men to graduate from these institutions. Given the low enrollment and success of Black men at HBCUs, Kimbrough and Harper (2006) asserted more research was needed on the experiences of Black men at these institutions. Since their clarion call, additional, but albeit limited, research has emerged on this demographic of students at HBCUs (Harper & Gasman, 2008; Lundy-Wagner & Gasman, 2011; Palmer & Gasman, 2008; Palmer & Strayhorn, 2008; Palmer & Wood, 2012). For example, Palmer et al. (2009) examined challenges to the retention and persistence for Black men at an HBCU and found that poor help-seeking behavior, lack of financial aid, and problems at home were salient challenges to the success of Black men. Furthermore, Harper and Gasman (2008) interviewed 76 Black men across 12

HBCUs and discovered that participants perceived the institutional climates of HBCUs as too conservative, resulting in an unwelcoming environment. Participants noted that conservatism was evident in sexuality and sexual orientation, self-presentation and expression, and ways in which faculty responded to students in the classroom.

Additional research on Black men at HBCUs suggests that these institutions need to be more proactive and intentional about understanding the contemporary experiences of Black men on their campuses (Kimbrough & Harper, 2006; Palmer & Maramba, 2012). For example, in a study, Kimbrough and Harper (2006) found that Black men had difficulty finding caring and committed mentors and role models at an HBCU. The participants noted that the few caring mentors and role models were sought by all the students, which created a burden on faculty and staff. In addition, participants also noted that women got preferential treatment from the overwhelmingly male professoriate because of their physical appearance. Similarly, in a study using Schlossberg's theory of mattering, Palmer and Maramba (2012) found that HBCUs could be more proactive in creating conditions of mattering to enhance persistence for Black men. Specifically, this study suggested that faculty could be more intentional in establishing relationships with Black males outside the classroom; they could be more flexible and understanding as they work with students; and they should go beyond lecturing in the classroom to actively engage Black male students.

Research has shown that HBCUs are very important institutions to higher education. Although fewer Black students are accessing these institutions today than in prior years, HBCUs continue to play an important role in the educational achievement of Black students. While this is the case, it is clear that more research on Black men at HBCUs is needed. In their chapter in Cuyjet's (2006) book, *African American Men in College*, Kimbrough and Harper (2006) asserted that researchers have focused so much attention on issues facing Black men at PWIs that the quality of life for Black students in general and Black men specifically at HBCUs has not received as much attention. Given this, additional research on Black men at HBCUs should focus on a range of issues that better help HBCU officials gain a better understanding of some of the core challenges to their retention and persistence. Not only should this research focus on Black men, but attention should be given to Black women as well. This research should employ diverse methodological approaches (i.e., qualitative, quantitative, or mixed methods) and focus on helping HBCUs implement best practices to increase student outcomes (Lundy-Wagner & Gasman, 2011; Palmer & Wood, 2012).

Black Men at Predominantly White Institutions

Although more Black students are now attending PWIs, they experience a chilly campus climate at these institutions (Allen, 1992; Cuyjet, 1997, 2006; Feagin, Vera, & Imani, 1996; Fries-Britt & Turner, 2001; Harper et al., 2011; Strayhorn, 2008c). Scholars have noted that Black men perceive PWIs to be hostile and unwelcoming, which stands in contrast to their experiences at HBCUs. Specifically, Black men at PWIs experience alienation (Feagin et al., 1996; Fries-Britt & Turner, 2002), have strained and unsupportive relationships with faculty (Guiffrida, 2005; Hurtado & Carter, 1997; Smedley, Myers, & Harrell, 1993), and are likely to view the curriculum as culturally exclusive.

Extant research indicates that faculty at PWIs have low expectations, biases, and prejudice regarding the intellectual abilities of Black men. According to Bonner and Bailey (2006), some faculty members perceive Black men as having poor academic socialization and low expectations for their educational success. Because of these experiences, many Black men have developed a "prove them wrong mentality." This psyche enables Black men to become even more determined and committed to their studies when they perceive there are doubts about their ability to be successful (Moore, Madison-Colmore, & Smith, 2003). Given the experiences that Black students have with faculty, they are more inclined to seek support from Black faculty, who they view as understanding, supportive, and demonstrating critical characteristics of othermothering (Guiffrida, 2005).

The competitive nature of the academic environment of PWIs serves as another challenge to the success of Black men. Bonner and Bailey (2006) noted that as Black men become socially integrated into the campus environment of PWIs, they often find themselves at odds with the cutthroat competition fostered by these institutions. These environments are less likely to produce the best learning outcomes for Black men, for whom social oriented academic climates are critical for learning and growth (Bonner & Bailey, 2006).

Interestingly, while research indicates that the sense of belonging for Black males hinges, in part, on interacting with peers from diverse racial and ethnic backgrounds (Strayhorn, 2008a), Harper and colleagues (2011) explained:

> *[The belongingness of Black men] is constantly threatened by the reinforcement of racist stereotypes that stigmatize them as unqualified admits who gained access to the institution through affirmative action or participation on an intercollegiate sports team, underprepared "at-risk" students who all emerged from low-income families and urban ghettos, and dangerous thugs from the local community who pose a security threat to the campus. (p. 180)*

These stereotypes, according to researchers (e.g., Harper & Kuykendall, 2012; Smith, Allen, & Danley, 2007; Strayhorn, 2008c), pose serious threats to the academic achievement of Black men at PWIs. For example, Harper and colleagues interviewed 52 Black male resident assistants from various PWIs and found that they experienced psychological stress from racist stereotypes and racial microaggressions, which caused them to limit their engagement in on-campus leadership activities, and in some cases, transfer to institutions with a more supportive campus climate. Other scholars have provided similar accounts of these experiences for Black men at PWIs (Cuyjet, 1997, 2006; Davis, 1994; Fries-Britt & Turner, 2001; Strayhorn, 2008c). Given the experiences of Black men at PWIs, these institutions must continue to improve the campus milieu so that Black students feel comfortable and supported to help facilitate their growth and development.

Black Men at Community Colleges

As noted in the first chapter, community colleges play a critical role in providing opportunities for Black men to access postsecondary education and many of the Black men in four-year colleges started off at community colleges. Notwithstanding, according to Flowers (2006), there are significant differences between Black men at four-year institutions and their counterparts in community colleges. Black male community college students are more likely to be older, married, have dependents, and to have delayed their enrollment into postsecondary education. They are also less likely to have higher degree expectations, to have graduated from private high schools, or to have enrolled in college preparation courses in foreign language, mathematics, and science (Wood, 2011). For many Black students, community colleges help facilitate their access to postsecondary educational opportunities (Bush & Bush, 2005; Wood, 2011, 2012; Wood & Turner, 2011). Nevertheless, a large number of Black men who begin their postsecondary education through community college do not persist to graduation or transfer to four-year institutions (Bush & Bush, 2005; Hagedorn et al., 2007; Strayhorn, 2011; Wood, 2011, 2012; Wood & Hilton, 2012b; Wood, Hilton, & Lewis, 2011; Wood & Turner, 2011). Black men are at an increased likelihood of prematurely departing from community college compared to men of other racial and ethnic groups (Hagedorn et al., 2007; Wood, 2011; Wood & Hilton, 2012b).

Evidence from Esters and Mosby (2007) documents the premature departure of Black men in community colleges. Specifically, using data from the Integrated Postsecondary Education Data System (IPEDS), they found that Black men have the lowest graduation rates compared to males from other racial/ethnic groups, with only 16% graduating in a three-year time span. Wood (2011) argued that Black males have the lowest mean grade point average (GPA) of men in community colleges. Using 2006 data from the U.S. Department of Education, Wood (2011) explained that White, Latino, and Asian American males had an average GPA of 2.90, 2.75, and 2.84, respectively, whereas Black men had a GPA of 2.64.

Despite these factors that negatively impact the success of Black males, scholars have identified other variables that are positively related to the success of these men in community colleges (e.g., Mosby, 2009; Rideaux, 2004; Strayhorn, 2011, 2012a; Wood, 2011, 2012, 2013; Wood & Williams, 2013). For example, while some research (e.g., Mason, 1994, 1998) has suggested that age is not a salient factor to the success of Black community college students, Hagedorn et al. (2007) found that younger students were more likely to persist than older students. Similarly, researchers (e.g., Mason, 1994; Stevens, 2006) have identified family support as critical to the success of Black men in community colleges. This research has found that when Black men receive family support, primarily from their mothers, their chances of succeeding were enhanced. Strayhorn (2011) noted the saliency of institutional satisfaction to the retention and persistence of Black community college students. Specifically, using data from 503 participants (65% women and 35% men) who completed the Community College Student Experiences Questionnaire (CCSEQ), he found that the age of Black students in community colleges was related to their level of satisfaction with their college experience. Strayhorn found that older students tend to be more satisfied with their experiences at community colleges than younger students. While he admitted that this finding contradicts research from prior studies (e.g., Hagedorn et al., 2007), he noted that this is an area in need of further examination. Strayhorn also found that Black students who were weighted down by family responsibilities were least satisfied with their experiences at community colleges.

In addition, research has identified faculty interaction as integral to the success of Black community college students (Bush & Bush, 2010; Wood, 2012). While Wood and Turner (2011) identified four factors critical to positive faculty–student interaction for Black male community students (e.g., friendly, displaying concern for students' performance, listening to students' concerns, and encouraging student to maximize their potential), research suggests that Black men in community college perceive faculty as unsupportive and not invested in their success (Bush & Bush, 2010; Wood, 2012). In spite of the fact that some research has provided critical context about the experiences of Black men in the community college, more research is needed to help provide insight into the experiences of this population. In fact, as a result of a comprehensive review of literature on Black men in community colleges, Wood and Hilton (2012a) found that less than eight peer-reviewed studies were published on Black male community college students from 1971 to 2009.

While many studies have focused on the experiences of Black men in higher education in recent years, further research is needed on the experiences of Black men in various institutional contexts, such as HBCUs and community colleges. More research is needed to help all institutions, specifically PWIs and community colleges, be more intentional about creating positive, affirming, and supportive campus ethos to help facilitate the success of Black men. Finally, more scholarly attention needs to focus on the within group differences among Black men. Scholars (e.g., Harper & Nichols, 2008; Palmer & Wood, 2012) have noted that Black men are not homogenous. By recognizing the intersectionalities among Black male college students, institutions will be better prepared to help them develop holistically and succeed academically (Palmer & Wood, 2012).

Student Engagement and Academic Success

Student engagement is defined as time and effort students devote to activities linked to desired outcomes (Kuh, 2009). It generally consists of students participating in meaningful activities and experiences, such as faculty–student collaboration, in-class discussions, peer interactions, and deep active learning (Strayhorn & DeVita, 2010). Although the definition of student engagement has evolved over time, for decades research has shown that students gain more out of their college experience when they devote time and energy to educational purposeful tasks (Kuh, 2009; Pace, 1990). In his theory of involvement, Astin (1984) emphasized the psychological and behavioral dimensions of being involved on campus and underscored the importance of involvement to student retention and persistence.

Research from numerous scholars has demonstrated a relationship between student engagement and outcomes, including cognitive development (Pascarella & Terenzini, 2005), psychological development (Chickering & Reisser, 1993), moral and ethnic development (Jones & Watt, 1999), and persistence (Berger & Milem, 1999). Flowers (2004) indicated that in-class and out-of-class engagement positively affected student development for 7,923 Black students who completed the College Student Experience Questionnaire (CSEQ). Similarly, Harper (2005) delineated the positive impact of campus engagement for high-achieving Black men who attended public research universities. Specifically, he explained that active engagement inside and outside of the classroom provided opportunities for these students to establish meaningful relationships with faculty and campus administrators, such as president, deans of students, and provost.

One of the primary benefits of campus engagement is an increased sense of belonging on campus. Sense of belonging is conceptualized as psychological processes connected with the students' adjustment and transition into college. Various types of social and academic integrations affect students' sense of belonging, which, in turn, affects their intention to persist (Hurtado & Carter, 1997; Strayhorn, 2012a). Schlossberg's (1989) work on mattering provides a lucid definition of belonging. Specifically, Schlossberg underscores the importance of students feeling like their presence on campus is noticed and valued by others, such as faculty, staff, and peers (Johnson et al., 2007). Given what we know about campus engagement and its many benefits (i.e., sense of belonging), this section will highlight factors that promote engagement on campus, which, in turn, influence sense of belonging for Black male college students. The specific factors discussed are: (a) student organizations, (b) faculty–student interaction, (c) peer interaction, (d) Black Greek Letter Fraternities, (e) Black Male Initiatives, and (f) mentors.

Student Organizations
Research has indicated a relationship between engaging in student organizations and institutional satisfaction for Black students (Cuyjet, 1997, 2006; Guiffrida, 2003; Harper, 2005, Harper & Quaye, 2007; Palmer & Wood, 2012; Patton, 2006; Strayhorn, 2012a). For example, Museus (2008) interviewed 24 students (12 Black students and 12 Asian American students) at a PWI and found that ethnic organizations served as spaces for cultural familiarity, cultural expression and advocacy, and cultural validation. While this research does not focus exclusively on Black men, it provides critical insight into spaces that promote student engagement and provides a safe space for Black students to connect with like-minded peers and establish meaningful relationships with key campus administrators.

Similarly in a study of 11 Black students (six men and five women) at a PWI, Patton (2006) explained that Black Cultural Centers not only provides a "home away from home" for Black students, but they also serve as a critical space where they can engage in educational purposeful activities, such as studying, interacting with peers, and holding meetings. These organizations also offer Black men critical opportunities to interact and establish meaningful relationships with minority faculty, staff, and students. Given the negative experiences many Black men encounter at PWIs, the relationships Black students have with these individuals are vital to helping Black men feel welcomed and valued and PWIs.

Harper and Quaye (2007) found that both predominantly Black and mainstream organizations provided Black men opportunities for engaging in social justice related activities, racial uplift, acquisition of cross-communication skills, and Black identity expression. Brown (2006) extended the conversation on ways that student organizations facilitate campus engagement for Black men. Specifically, as a result of interviewing 25 Black men at a PWI, he reported that intramural athletics and recreational activities, student unions, and mentoring that encouraged cocurricular involvement are important spaces that help to create opportunities for Black male campus engagement. Some of Brown's findings are noteworthy and complimentary to Cuyjet's (1997) and Kimbrough and Harper's (2006) work on Black men. Specifically, Cuyjet as well as Kimbrough and Harper noted that Black men are more likely to participate in athletics and recreational activities.

Despite the many benefits students derived from being engaged on campus, Black men are generally disengaged on the campuses of PWIs and HBCUs. In community colleges, Flowers (2006) found that Black men were less integrated academically and socially than their same race counterparts in four-year institutions, indicating a need to increase campus engagement for Black male community college students. Given this, institutions have to be more intentional about understanding what factors are more likely to promote Black male engagement on campus. Palmer and Young (2009) suggested that universities consider surveying Black men to understand what their interests are and implement educational purposeful activities that will encourage their engagement on campus. While literature has provided some insight into Black male engagement on campus, more research is needed to increase campus engagement among this demographic.

Faculty–Student Interaction

In addition to student organizations, faculty–student interaction helps to facilitate campus engagement. Indeed research has been unequivocal in its assertion between meaningful faculty–student interaction and student learning and personal development (Astin, 1993; Chickering & Reisser, 1993; Kuh & Hu, 2001; Tinto, 1993). Extant research has shown a relationship between faculty interaction and multiple educational gains, including academic skill development, leadership ability, occupational values, and gains in educational aspirations (Sax, Bryant, & Harper, 2005). The more contact students have with faculty inside as well as outside the classroom, the greater their gains will be with student development and institutional satisfaction (Astin, 1993). Tinto (1993) argued that the more students are engaged in the institution, the more likely that they will experience opportunities to development meaningful interactions with faculty, which will increase their sense of belonging and positively impact their retention and persistence.

Though faculty interaction helps to facilitate multiple outcomes, satisfaction with faculty relationships vary by race (Lundberg & Schreiner, 2004). For example, White students report having the greatest satisfaction with faculty relationships while the opposite is true for Black students (Davis, 1994; Feagin et al., 1996; Fleming, 1984; Fries-Britt & Turner, 2002; Guiffrida, 2005). Although recent research has shown that Black men experience unique challenges (e.g., Kimbrough & Harper, 2006; Palmer & Maramba, 2012) with faculty at HBCUs, an overwhelming amount of literature suggests that Black men have nurturing and welcoming relationships with faculty (Fleming, 1984; Fries-Britt & Turner, 2002; Palmer & Gasman, 2008; Palmer & Wood, 2012). Similar to their counterparts in PWIs, Black men perceive faculty in community colleges to be unsupportive and apathetic toward their success (Bush & Bush, 2010; Wood, 2012). In sum, given the critical role faculty play in student success in postsecondary education, more effort must be devoted to ensuring that faculty are student-centered. To help faculty develop this sense of student centeredness, institutions should hold workshops and consider studying institutions, such as HBCUs, that have a reputation of hiring faculty who go above and beyond the call of duty to help maximize student success.

Peer Interaction

Peer interaction influences campus engagement among students (Astin, 1993; Bonner & Bailey, 2006; Harper, 2006b; Tinto, 1993). By interacting with peers, students have greater exposure to campus resources and student organizations, and develop a social network that can be critical in helping them navigate academic and nonacademic dilemmas (Astin, 1993; Bonner & Bailey, 2006; Tinto, 1993). Astin (1993) explained, "The single most powerful source on influence on the undergraduate student's academic and personal development is the peer group . . . the amount of interaction among peers has far reaching effects on nearly all areas of student learning and development" (p. 8). For Black students in higher education, peer groups play an even greater role because they help to facilitate a sense of belonging in an institutional milieu that differs significantly from "their ethnic, cultural, and socioeconomic background" (Bonner & Bailey, 2006, p. 26).

According to Astin (1993), peer interaction facilitates academic development, problem-solving skills, critical thinking, and cultural awareness for Black men in particular. Other scholars (Davis, 1999; Harper, 2006b, 2013; Palmer & Gasman, 2008; Strayhorn, 2008a) support the relationship between peer interaction and a wide range of academic and social gains for Black men. In a study of 32 high-achieving Black male college students, Harper (2006b) reported that participants' same race peers helped to support, encourage, and validate their academic success. Similarly, Palmer and Gasman (2008) found that relationships with like-minded peers, who were focused on succeeding academically, had a positive impact on the success of 11 Black men at an HBCU.

Interestingly, while research has shown that Black students were less likely to interact with White peers outside of the classroom because of discriminatory behavior they have experienced from some members of this population (Davis, 1994; Feagin et al., 1996), Strayhorn (2008a) found that cross-racial peer interactions facilitated the sense of belonging for Black males. In particular, he indicated that interactions with someone of a diverse background or perspective can lead to meaningful interactions that help to foster greater sense of belonging to the institution. Despite finding that cross-racial peer interactions were significant predictors of sense of belonging for both Black and White male college students, Strayhorn posited that this topic warranted further investigation. Strayhorn's findings indicate the need for colleges and universities to be more intentional about fostering a campus climate where students feel encouraged to develop meaningful relationships with peers of diverse racial and cultural backgrounds. In fact, Palmer, Maramba, and Holmes (2011) noted that because students want to be prepared to compete in today's global economy, they want to have more meaningful exchanges with peers of different races and ethnic backgrounds. However, they expressed that educational institutions do little to promote such interaction. While a copious body of literature has provided some perspective about the outcomes associated with peer interactions for Black men across a variety of educational types (e.g., PWIs and HBCUs), a paucity of research has discussed ways in which peer interaction affects success for Black men in community colleges. For example, Poole (2006) identified peer support as vital to the success of Black men in community colleges, noting that these relationships help to improve their academic and social integration. Furthermore, Bush and Bush (2010) explained that peer interaction plays a critical role in helping to determine GPA, transfer, and degree/certificate attainment for Black male community college students. Despite this, in a study of 87 men of color across four community colleges, 42% of whom were Black men, Gardenhire-Crooks, Collado, Martin, and Castro (2010) found that many males felt that forming friendships on campus could be a liability rather than an asset to their academic success.

Black Greek Letter Fraternities

Aside from peer interaction, Black Greek Letter Fraternities (BGLFs) have been showed to facilitate campus engagement (Kimbrough, 1995, 1997, 2003). Despite the fact that BGLFs have generated negative publicity because of hazing (Kimbrough, 1995, 1997, 2003) and have been accused of promoting self-segregations (McClure, 2006; Taylor & Howard-Hamilton, 1995), BGLFs have been shown to be critical contributors to the growth and development of Black men (Kimbrough, 1995, 1997; Kimbrough

& Hutcheson, 1998). For example, using a two-part questionnaire that examined the perception of leadership skills and participation in leadership activities for 61 Black male students (27 of whom were affiliated in BGLFs and 34 were members of other Black student groups on campus) at a rural PWI, Kimbrough (1995) found that while both groups (members of BGLFs as well as members of other student organizations) held similar views of leaderships, BGLFs served as a vital source for opportunities for leadership development. Kimbrough's findings are consistent with other researchers (McClure, 2006; Sutton & Kimbrough, 2001).

In addition to helping Black men develop leadership skills, BGLFs also facilitate racial identity development because members of BGLFs are actively engaged in in- and out-of-classroom activities that impact the social and cultural well-being of Black individuals on and off campus (Harper & Harris, 2006). Research has shown that members of BGLFs are focused on the collective responsibility for Blacks in general and Black students on campus specifically (Harper, 2008). This sense of collective responsibility serves as the impetus for members of BGLFs to not only serve as a positive representation of their organizations, but also act as role models for Black students on campus (Harper, 2008).

As noted, BGLFs are particularly important for Black men at PWIs. For example, Harper and Harris (2006) explained that BGLFs provide social programming for Black students at PWIs that would not otherwise exist, which helps to increase Black male social engagement and institutional satisfaction. Similarly, Sutton and Kimbrough (2001) reported that BGLFs engender sense of belonging for Black men and provide opportunities for them to gain transferable leadership and communications skills. In sum, while some have questioned the relevancy of BGLFs in the 21st century, this research reveals that these organizations are still vital to the growth and development of Black male college students. Given this, institutions have to find meaningful ways to work with these organizations to promote Black male engagement and facilitate their belongingness on campus while encouraging members of BGLFs to engage in safe and responsible behavior during member in-take sessions.

Black Male Initiatives

Black Male Initiatives (BMIs) have also been showed to facilitate Black male campus engagement (Bledsoe & Rome, 2006; Bonner & Bailey, 2006; Harper & Harris, 2012; Palmer, Maramba, & Dancy, 2013; Wood & Palmer, 2012). Although there are many types of BMIs implemented across diverse institutional types, there are some core commonalities among them. Many BMIs are research-based in that program development and implementation are informed by extant research and theory. To this end, they function to foster academic and social integration, student engagement, sense of belonging, and create a welcoming and affirming campus environment for Black men. Second, they have a focus on collectivity, as exemplified through program slogans, mottos, and themes. Collectivity suggests that successes and failures are mutually shared. Under this, value, collaboration, community, otherness, and equity are important virtues. Third, through formal and informal mentor models, BMIs facilitate faculty-to-student, student-to-student, and student-to-youth mentoring. Fourth, many BMIs have programming designed to facilitate students' critical reflection of their personal, academic, and professional goals and philosophical outlook on life. These reflections are facilitated by journaling as well as small and large group discussions.

Though diverse in nature, BMIs provide a safe place for Black men to discuss a range of issues, from academic to social experiences. They have also been critical in helping increase their retention and persistence (Bledsoe & Rome, 2006; Bonner & Bailey, 2006) at HBCUs (Palmer et al., 2013; Wood & Palmer, 2012). Further, research has shown that BMIs help normalize the importance of Black men relying not only on each other for support, but also the larger campus system (Palmer et al., 2009, 2013). This is important because research has illustrated that pride often keeps Black men from using external academic and social services on campus for help when they encounter difficulties and challenges (Majors & Billson, 1992; Palmer et al., 2009, 2013). While evidence indicates that community colleges have retention programs and BMIs to help facilitate the success of Black men (Wood, 2011; Wood & Harris, 2013), there is little research (e.g., Nevarez & Wood, 2010) to assess the efficacy of these programs. Given this, more research is needed on the outcomes of these programs at community colleges.

Mentors

In addition to Black Male Initiatives, mentors are critical to the success of Black men in postsecondary education. Mentors on campus can act as powerful agents that help to encourage Black male campus engagement (Cuyjet, 1997, 2006; Harper, 2012; LaVant, Anderson, & Tiggs, 1997; Strayhorn, 2008c; Sutton, 2006). For example, Scott (2012) discussed the importance of mentors on campus, suggesting that they can serve to create a welcoming and affirming campus climate. Specifically, he noted that mentors can be responsible for (a) acclimating students to the campus environment; (b) informing students about campus involvement (e.g., clubs, organizations, activities) and professional opportunities (e.g., internships); and (c) serving as guides as students continue through college. Similarly, Harper (2012) discussed the many ways that upperclassmen served as mentors to freshmen by helping them become academically and socially integrated into the campus. Specifically, the mentors shared critical insight and important knowledge about resources, helped connect the students to invaluable information networks, and introduced them to engagement opportunities on campus. At HBCUs, faculty members serve as a vital source of mentoring for Black men (Berger & Milem, 2000; Fries-Britt & Turner, 2002; Gasman, 2008; Palmer & Gasman, 2008; Wagener & Nettles, 1998). Professors at HBCUs are often credited with going above and beyond their professional responsibilities to help nurture and support the academic success and social development of Black students. While on-campus mentors are salient to the success of Black men, mentors and role models off campus also provide a rich source of support for Black men (Cuyjet, 1997, 2006; Palmer & Gasman, 2008; Scott, 2012; Wood & Palmer, 2012).

In sum, research has identified salient factors that help to promote campus engagement for Black men in higher education. Campus engagement is associated with a variety of outcomes, including increased sense of belonging and persistence. Despite the factors that help to promote campus engagement for Black men, many of these students are disengaged on the campuses of PWIs, HBCUs, and community colleges. While the factors highlighted in this section are critical to the success of Black men in higher education, we grouped these factors together because of their commonality in helping to promote campus engagement for Black men. In the subsequent section, we discuss other factors integral to the success of Black men in postsecondary education.

Factors Critical to the Success of Black Men in Postsecondary Education

In this section, we draw attention to additional factors vital to the success of Black male college students: (a) financial support, (b) spirituality, (c) family support, (d) non-cognitive factors, (e) racial identity, and (f) masculine identity.

Financial Support

Many researchers (e.g., Heller, 2003; Perna, 2006; St. John, 2002; St. John, Hu, & Weber, 2001; St. John, Paulsen, & Starkey, 1996; St. John & Starkey, 1995; Swail et al., 2003; Titus, 2006; Wood et al., 2011) have found that financial factors are one of the most important predictors of decisions to leave college for minority students. In fact, research shows that concerns about financing college plays a critical role in where students decide to attend college (St. John, 2002; St. John & Starkey, 1995; St. John et al., 1996, 2001). For example, many minority students generally enroll in community colleges (National Center for Public Policy and Higher Education, 2011) and public HBCUs because they are seen as low cost options (Palmer et al., 2009). Further while evidence suggests that financial aid is critical to the success of Black college students, some types have a positive influence and others have a questionable impact. For example, gifts in the form of scholarships and grants have been linked to higher rates of persistence and degree attainment for Black students (St. John, 2002; Swail et al., 2003; U.S. GAO, 1995). One analysis revealed that an additional $1,000 in grants lowered the probability of Black and Hispanic students leaving college by 7%–8% (U.S. GAO, 1995). Nevertheless, even with financial aid, Black students from low-income families are less likely than students from higher socioeconomic status to enroll in a four-year institution and complete a baccalaureate degree (Swail et al., 2003).

The influence of loans appears to be more complex, with researchers finding loan amounts to be both positively and negatively correlated with success. While more research is needed to make sense of these conflicting results, what is evident is that loans appear to promote success among White students more effectively than minorities (U.S. GAO, 1995). This could be due to the fact that Black students are more sensitive to college costs and more averse to taking out loans to finance their college education (Ehrenberg, 1991; Kaltenbaugh, St. John, & Starkey, 1999). Regardless of the reason for the differential effects of loans on college degree attainment, the fact that loans might not be as likely to increase success among Black students is critical, given that policymakers have increasingly relied on loans in the composition of financial aid packages (St. John, 2003; Wei & Carroll, 2004). Moreover, even when Black students rely on loans to support their education, when policymakers make changes to the requirements to receive loans, some students have been less likely to be awarded the loans, which complicate their success. For example, the recent modifications to the requirements for the Parent PLUS loan (PPL) have caused many low-income students to be denied the PPL, which has severely affected student enrollment and persistence at HBCUs (Libby, 2012).

There is evidence that employment influences success for college students, but that impact depends on the location and nature of work. Extant research on college student population suggests that working off campus is negatively associated with success—especially working more than 25 hours per week off campus (Pascarella, Edison, Nora, Hagedorn, & Terenzini, 1998). Conversely, existing empirical evidence appears to suggest that working on campus can positively influence success (Kuh, Kinzie, Buckley, Bridges, & Hayek, 2007). This being the case, the inability to pay for college, insufficient financial resources, or the need to financially support their family back home may force many Black males to work a substantial number of hours while attempting to attend college full time, thereby adversely affecting their likelihood of success. Researchers have revealed that, due to inadequate finances, many minority students in general need to have a job to compensate for their school and living expenses (e.g., Branch-Brioso, 2009; Green & Glasson, 2009).

While evidence indicate that nearly 84% of community college students hold some form of employment during college (Wood et al., 2011), given the economic downturn, the need to work while in college may have increased among most students in higher education, especially those who are low-income minority students. Due to the need to work, many minority students are more attracted to for-profit institutions than the traditional institutions of higher education because they offer greater flexibility to take classes (Bennett, Lucchesi, & Vedder, 2010; Rooks, 2013). In fact, Rooks (2013) stated that from 2004 to 2010, Black enrollment in for-profit bachelor degree programs grew by 218% compared to a modest increase of 24% at public four-year colleges and universities. As a result, the two top producers of baccalaureate degrees for Black students in 2011 were for-profit institutions (i.e., University of Phoenix and Ashford University).

In sum, the ability to pay for college is a major factor influencing the success of Black men. Rising college costs and trends toward increased reliance on loans in the composition of financial aid packages all contribute to financial pressures for Black students. While students can work to compensate for inadequate finances, working too many hours can also hinder their success.

Spirituality

Another key factor to the success of Black men in higher education is spirituality. Researchers have defined spirituality in various ways. For example, Mattis (2000) indicated that spirituality includes a belief in having a personal relationship with God and living according to God's will. On the other hand, Love and Talbot (1999) noted that spirituality involves the pursuit of discovering meaning and purpose in one's life. Extant literature has suggested a relationship between spirituality and retention for Black male college students (Dancy, 2010a; Herndon, 2003; Watson, 2006). For example, Herndon (2003) conducted a study with 13 Black male students and found that spirituality was critical to the success of participants. Specifically, he noted that spirituality bolstered their resiliency, provided a sense of purpose, and augmented the support that participants received from religious institutions. While Wood and Hilton (2012b) have reported similar findings for Black men in community colleges, using Armstrong Measure of Spirituality with 125 Black students, Weddle-West, Hagan, and Norwood (2013) found that Black men at HBCUs scored significantly lower on the spiritual belief variable than Black men and women at PWIs. Given the challenges that Black students face at PWIs, Weddle-West et al. concluded that Black students at these institutions may need to rely more on spirituality as a coping mechanism than students at HBCUs.

Family Support

In addition to spirituality, research has identified family as important to the success of Black men in higher education. Interestingly, in Tinto's theory of student departure, he urged students transitioning from high school to college to divorce themselves from their past communities, including friends and family to become academically and socially integrated into the college milieu (Tinto, 1993). Despite this, researchers have noted that for minority students, family plays an important role in their persistence (Guiffrida, 2004; Hurtado, Carter, & Spuler, 1996; Nora & Cabrera, 1996; Rosas & Hamrick, 2002). For example, in a qualitative study of 50 Black students (24 of whom were men), Barnett (2004) found that participants' families played a critical role in their success by decreasing stress and serving as an emotional outlet. Similarly, Palmer, Davis, and Maramba (2011) explained that family served as a critical factor to the success of 11 Black men at an HBCU. Specifically, Palmer et al. indicated that although some of the participants' family members lacked formal education, they provided inspirational and encouraging messages that had a significant impact on the participants' success.

While evidence illustrates ways in which families can be supportive of the success of minorities, Guiffrida (2004) noted that families could also be assets or liabilities to the success of Black students. In a study of 99 Black students, which consisted of 15 students who left the university prematurely (leavers), 65 academically low-achieving students (low achievers), and 19 high-achieving students (high achievers), Guiffrida found that while the high achievers received emotional and academic support from their families, the leavers felt that their families contributed to emotional strain because of family circumstances, which contributed to their poor academic performance. Similarly, Guiffrida indicated that while the high achievers received financial support from their families, leavers wished that their families would have helped them, and in some cases, felt guilty for taking money away from their struggling families.

While research has shown a relationship between family support and academic success for Black males, some research has suggested that if Black males enrolled in community colleges are overwhelmed with family responsibilities (Strayhorn, 2011), this could impede their success. Similarly, Wood (2011) found that family responsibilities were likely to hinder the success of Black men who recently enrolled in community college compared to those who made progress toward their degree. Perhaps this finding might indicate that Black men who have made progress toward their degrees and who have families have learned to adjust to the responsibilities of having a family compared to Black men recently enrolled in community colleges.

Non-cognitive Factors

Non-cognitive skills are those attitudes, behaviors, and strategies (e.g., motivation, perseverance, and self-control) which facilitate success. These factors are coined "non-cognitive" because they are distinct from the cognitive skills measured by tests (Gutman & Schoon, 2013). Scholars have indicated that non-cognitive factors have particular relevance to the success of Black students in higher education (Cokley, 2003; Moore, 2001; Moore et al., 2003; Swail et al., 2003; Wood & Harris, 2013). For example, Tracey and Sedlacek (1985) identified eight non-cognitive factors integral to the success of Black students at PWIs. While these factors range from positive self-concept to successful leadership experience, Tracey and Sedlacek (1985) indicated that one critical non-cognitive factor for Black students at PWIs is the ability to deal with racism.

Furthermore, scholars have identified strong study habits and time management skills as being salient to the success of Black students (Hrabowski et al., 1998). Moore (2001) argued, "success in college has less to do with aptitude in cognitive measures . . . than non-cognitive measures such as self-efficacy, motivation, commitment, and persistence" (p. 77). In his study of

140 Black male college students, Strayhorn (2013c) actualized Moore's quote by noting the role that grit (i.e., persistence, determination, and motivation) played in their success at a PWI. While researchers (e.g., Palmer & Strayhorn, 2008; Wood & Palmer, 2013) have underscored the relationship between non-cognitive factors and success for Black men at HBCUs and community colleges, Palmer and Strayhorn (2008) noted that the institutions still have a responsibility to provide the resources to support student success.

Racial Identity

Racial identity is another non-cognitive factor researchers have linked to the success of Black men in higher education (Cokley, 2001; Hrabowski et al., 1998; Lott, 2011; Okech & Harrington, 2002). Black racial identity is rooted in William E. Cross's model of nigrescence (i.e., the process of becoming Black). Cross's model consists of several stages, which explains how Blacks move from a White frame of reference to a positive Black frame of reference (Lott, 2011). His model comprises the following phases: (a) preencounter, (b) encounter, (c) immersion–emersion, and (d) internalization. The initial stage (i.e., preencounter) indicates that Blacks generally engage in a process of self-loathing while simultaneously valuing White values and ways. As the stages progress, Blacks internalize a more positive racial identity and learn to embrace elements of biculturalism and multiculturalism (Lott, 2011).

Nasim, Roberts, Hamell, and Young (2005) conducted a longitudinal study with 250 Black students attending a PWI and an HBCU in order to investigate the relationship between positive racial identity and academic success. Findings from their study revealed a relationship between a positive racial identity and performing well in school. In his study of 190 Black men attending five research universities, Reid (2013) found similar results. Specifically, he found that Black men with high GPAs were not only academically and socially integrated into college, but also held positive racial identity beliefs. His findings are supported by Hrabowski et al. (1998) who found that high-achieving Black men possessed both a positive racial identification and a positive male identification. While research supports a linkage between positive racial identity and academic success, Campbell and Fleming (2000) found the inverse for Black male students with weak racial identity. Specifically, in a study of 141 Black males attending a largely minority urban university, they discovered that Black males who feared success had a weak or conflicted racial identity. In the context of this study, Campbell and Fleming (2000) defined fear of success as "feelings of anxiety which arise as an individual approaches the accomplishment of important, self-defined goals, the attainment of which is both deeply desired and resisted by the individual" (p. 5).

While most research (e.g., Hrabowski et al., 1998; Reid, 2013) has shown a relationship between positive racial identity and academic success, some literature has linked racial identity to sense of belonging for Black students at PWIs. Specifically, research has suggested that Black students with a positive racial identity are more likely to feel connected to the institution (Mitchell & Dell, 1992; Taylor & Howard-Hamilton, 1995). For example, Parker and Flowers (2003) administered the Racial Identity Attitude Scale to 118 Black students (59% men and 41% women) to assess the effects of racial identity on their GPA and sense of belonging. While they did not find a relationship between racial identity and GPA, they found a relationship between racial identity and students' sense of belonging on campus. Clearly more research is needed to better understand the relationship between racial identity and academic achievement. However, given that some research has found a link between racial identity and sense of belonging, practitioners should consider holding workshops, forums, and other programmatic initiatives to help Black men (particular at PWIs) enhance their sense of racial identity, which might positively impact their sense of belonging.

Masculine Identity
Although we broached the topic of Black boys and masculinities in the second chapter, we continue this conversation in this chapter because we recognize that it is critical to understand Black men as gendered beings in order to help increase their academic and social development in higher education (Dancy, 2010b, 2011; Davis, 1999, 2012; Harper, 2004; Harris & Harper, 2008; Harris, Palmer, & Struve, 2011). Scholars have noted that engaging in campus activities, developing meaningful friendships and interpersonal relationships, and seeking support when needed are indicative of healthy psychological development for college men. However, men are less

inclined to engage in these behaviors "because they are traditionally defined as feminine and conflict with lessons about masculinity prior to college" (Harris & Harper, 2008, p. 29).

Majors and Billson (1992) proposed the concept of cool pose to understand patterns of masculine expression among Black men of all ages. They argued that cool pose is a strategy that Black men use to cope with oppression and social alienation. Black men express cool pose "through styles of speaking, gesturing, dressing, wearing hair, walking, standing, and shaking hands. The ritualized acts are directed at the dominant culture and allow Black men to express pride, strength, and control in opposition to White male masculine norms" (Harris et al., 2011, p. 50). Some assert that cool pose causes Black men to divorce themselves from activities associated with White and feminine values, such as education and to place greater emphasis on pursuits, such as music, athletics, and entertainment (Corbin & Pruitt, 1999; Harris et al., 2011; Jackson & Moore, 2008; Palmer et al., 2009). Similarly, others have argued that cool pose causes Black men to express masculinities by emphasizing sexual promiscuity, toughness, and physical expressions (Majors & Billson, 1992; Majors, Tyler, Peden, & Hall, 1994; Stinson, 2006).

In addition to cool pose, some Black men may experience male gender role conflict (MGRC), which is psychological and emotional anxiety resulting "from men's fear of femininity and inability to live up to socially constructed masculinities" (Harris et al., 2011, p. 50). When men are unable to conform to the hegemonic expectations of what it means to be a man, they may view themselves as less masculine and assume others will hold similar views. While research has identified cool pose and MGRC to explain expression of masculinities among Black men, Martin and Harris (2006) contributed to the discourse on this topic by adding a more nuanced perspective on men and masculinities. Specifically they interviewed 27 "academically driven" student-athletes to understand their beliefs about masculinities. The participants in their study associated masculinities with being accountable, displaying character, serving communities and pursing academic excellence.

Similarly, Harper (2004) investigated expressions of masculinities for 32 high-achieving Black men enrolled in six PWIs with high GPAs and lengthy records of leadership and involvement on campus. Participants in his study expressed concepts of masculinities that differed significantly from Black males uninvolved on campus. Harper explained that while high-achieving Black men expressed masculinities by pursuing academic excellence, becoming leaders on campus, and serving the Black communities, the participants' same-race uninvolved peers' conceptualized masculinities by pursuing short-term sexual relationships with women, competing in male-dominated activities, and accumulating and displaying material wealth.

Black men's conceptualization and expression of masculinities change as they grow and mature in life (Kimmel & Messner, 2007). College educators need to understand that not all Black men express masculinities consistently and that they can play a critical role in helping men develop a healthy gender identity (Harris et al., 2011). Despite the critical nature of this research, limited research has provided context regarding how Black men at community college express masculinities (Gardenhire-Crooks et al., 2010; Harris & Harper, 2008). For example, Harris and Harper explained Black men in community college may be more prone to MGRC. Similarly, a dearth of research exists to explain ways in which Black men at HBCUs express masculinities. For example, Dancy (2011) examined ways in which PWIs and HBCUs developed expectations of masculinities for 24 Black men enrolled across 12 universities. Dancy noted that the Black men at HBCUs felt pressured to live up to the media's depictions of Black men (i.e., rap artists, athletes, criminals), which they believed the Black community valued in Black men's manhood. Participants also felt pressured to conform to hegemonic notions of manhood. Given the paucity of research, additional knowledge that provides deeper insight into ways that Black men conceptualize masculinities in both of these institutional contexts is warranted (i.e., HBCUs and community colleges). In summary, a number of factors help to contribute to the success of Black men in higher education. Being aware of these factors could play a vital role in helping educators, researchers, administrators, and policymakers enhance success for Black male college students.

Conclusion

Extant research has illustrated that given the precollege experiences of many Black men they must depend on a number of initiatives to help facilitate their access to higher education. Despite the critical roles of these initiatives, some are gradually being reduced or dismantled, which will pose significant challenges to the ability of Black men to access postsecondary education. In order to help increase college access among Black men, serious attention and resources must be devoted to improving their precollege experience. Furthermore, stakeholders, faculty, and researchers must place more attention on advocating for the functionality of these critical programs that acts as a gateway for Black men to enter higher education.

Similarly, research has provided critical insight into the experiences of Black men across diverse institutional types; however, further research is needed to help these institutions be more intentional about promoting success among Black males. While this is true of all institutional types, given the experiences that Black men have on the campuses of PWIs, and, to some extent, community colleges, these institutions must focus intently on ways to increase mattering for Black males on their campuses. Finally, this chapter has revealed the importance of campus engagement for Black males and discussed its impact on influencing a variety of outcomes, including sense of belonging. Notwithstanding, campus engagement among Black men is woefully low across all institutional types. College educators, researchers, and administrators must be more cognizant about finding creative and innovative ways to help facilitate campus engagement among this demographic of students.

Implications for Future Research, Policy, and Practice

M ANY BLACK MALE CHILDREN are at risk of educational failure as a result of a complex array of institutional and socioeconomic factors they face within their schools, colleges, and the communities in which they live. These current social and educational conditions have historical roots and persist across generations. Effective policies and innovative interventions are needed to improve the plight of Black boys and men in educational settings and society. Guided by this notion, here we use the literature examined in previous chapters to highlight implications for future research, practice, and policy.

Implications for Future Research

Our preceding literature review has several implications for future research. First, while there is some research on how school contexts affect Black male educational and social experiences, future research should focus on the interaction of school contexts (i.e., single-sex schools) and aspects of self (e.g., masculine identity). An array of strategies has captured the attention of school administrators, local communities, and parents as possible solutions to the problems associated with Black males in public schools. These strategies are of two primary programmatic genres: assistive/supportive and reconstructive (Brown, Dancy, & Davis, 2007; Davis, 1999). Assistive/supportive programs aim to support current school structures by providing Black male youth with the positive presence of adult Black men in school settings. Mentoring programs that assign Black male professionals as role models for young boys, typically in elementary and middle schools, have been established in many school districts, both urban and suburban. Similarly, Black men have been enlisted to serve as teacher's aids, tutors, and reading partners for Black boys needing academic support and guidance.

The justification for these initiatives points to the need in educational settings for consistent, positive adult males who can provide role models for young Black males to emulate (Canada, 1998). These programs attempt to counter the negative gender-role socialization of Black males that is peer-inspired that too often leads to maladaptive masculine identity (Winbush, 2001). Their objective is to develop conceptions and expressions of masculinity that are not antithetical to high-achievement behaviors and attitudes. The goal of reconstructive programs is to develop conceptions and expressions of masculinity that are not antithetical to high-achievement behaviors and attitudes. Reconstructive programs focus intensely on self-esteem and ethnic identity and include initiatives such as masculine identity development programs (i.e., pathways to manhood, rites of passage).

Second, within a broader framework, it is clear that problems observed within schools and colleges are not always institutional problems per se. Historical and ongoing inequality in society and institutionalized racism largely keep well-intentioned reform agendas from reaching Black males. The criminalization of Black boys and men, such as in racial profiling, the continual disparaging media images challenged by the National Association for the Advancement of Colored People, and the overrepresentation of Black men in state and federal prisons are phenomena that are inextricably linked to educational at-risk conditions. The strategies often used in primary and secondary school reform represent a responsible but incomplete approach to addressing the needs of Black male adolescents (Jordan & Cooper, 2003). Similarly, in postsecondary education, approaches to advancing Black male achievement (though well intentioned) have failed to adequately address their needs.

Stone (1997) defines security as "protecting people's identities as well as their existence" (p. 90). Although often disregarded, needs are critical components of schools, and they must first ensure that all reasonable student needs are met or accommodated. Hence, any examination of student achievement must necessarily include an investigation of student needs. This line of reasoning raises the question: Do Black students, especially males but indeed all students, have access to meaningful networks, adequate resources, and enriching opportunities—their most basic academic needs? As Anyon (1995) argued, endeavoring to reform schools without simultaneously strengthening the community in which they are located is like attempting to filter the air in a room with the windows open (Anyon, 1995). The community is the whole and the school is the fragment (Jordan & Cooper, 2003). However, educational politics, complex bureaucracy, and institutionalism shape a narrow-minded view of schools and schooling that shamefully shows little attention to the demographics and cultural backgrounds of the student population.

Third, as noted, this monograph focused on the experiences of Black men in diverse institutional types. As scholars who have made important contributions to the literature on Black men in HBCUs, PWIs, and community colleges, we felt that employing this approach was critical because Black men in each of these institutional contexts have unique characteristics, experiences, and circumstances that shape and inform their ability to persist to graduation. In reviewing literature for this monograph, we noted that over the years, researchers have devoted significant time and attention to examining the experiences of Black men at PWIs, but failed to devote equal attention to the experiences of Black men in other contexts. For example, Wood and Hilton (2012a) found that less than eight peer-reviewed studies were published on Black male community college students from 1971 to 2009. While additional research has emerged on Black men in community colleges in the last few years, more research is needed to help faculty, institutional administrators, student affairs professionals, and policymakers have a more informed understanding of the experiences of Black male community college students. Enhanced understanding of these experiences can lead to improved policies, programs, and practices that can advance Black male retention and attainment.

Similarly, additional research is needed on Black men at HBCUs. While the literature on HBCUs is replete with empirical evidence of the relevancy of HBCUs to the landscape of American higher education, relatively little research has focused on the experiences Black men within these institutional contexts. Although fewer Black students are attending HBCUs than in the past, these institutions continue to serve as a critical source of access to higher education for Black students particularly, those of whom who are low-income and academically underprepared specifically. In 2006, Kimbrough and Harper stressed the need for more scholarly inquiry about the experiences of Black men at HBCUs. Nevertheless the higher education research community has been slow to respond to this call. Turning more research attention to Black men at HBCUs will likely offer greater insight into programmatic initiatives, strategies, and policies that help to facilitate the success of Black men at these institutions.

Furthermore, as noted in the first chapter of this monograph, a large and growing portion of Black men access higher education through for-profit institutions. Despite this, only one scholarly resource to date (see Fountaine, 2012) has examined the experiences of Black men within these contexts. To this end, we were not able to devote significant scholarly treatment to Black men in for-profit institutions in the third chapter. However, we urge future researchers to consider Black men who seek access to higher education through these venues as their experiences may be qualitatively different from those who attend other not-for-profit institutions. This is a critical and urgent need given the high tuition and fees, loan default rates, and unemployment of students attending for-profit colleges (e.g., Miller & Mupinga, 2006; Mullin, 2010; Riegg, 2006). In recognizing and advocating for additional research on Black men in diverse institutional types, we are not encouraging researchers to forfeit focusing on Black men in one institutional type over the other. However, we realize that research on Black men can be best utilized when it is uniquely situated in the institutional context in which Black students are enrolled.

In addition to this, this monograph (based on the landscape of prior research) treated Black men as a homogenous group; however, research on this student demographic can be best applied and used more effectively when it takes into consideration the within-group differences of Black men. In their book, *Black Men in College: Implications for HBCUs and Beyond*, Palmer and Wood (2012) strongly urge future research to avoid monolithic depictions of Black males in postsecondary education. They emphasized that intersectionalities must be addressed with respect to student characteristics (e.g., class, age, sexual orientation, immigrant status), parental and family attributes (e.g., parent's highest level of education, dependency status), religion (e.g., religious affiliation, religiosity, spirituality), regional differences (e.g., southern, western, eastern, midwestern), environmental characteristics (e.g., employment status, peer influences), campus involvement (e.g., Greeks, student leaders), institutional type (e.g., two-year, four-year), and control (e.g., public, private not-for-profit, private for-profit), all of which are illustrated in Strayhorn's (2013b) recent volume on intersectionality and Black collegians. We agree with Palmer and Wood's sentiment and feel that placing more emphasis on the heterogeneity of Black men will lead to revised models and theories, and offer unique insights about Black men in postsecondary education.

Another area where additional research is needed is effective alliances between higher education and the preK–12 contexts. In the second chapter, we noted that programs that promote access to postsecondary education for Black men are critical given the inequalities that Black students experience in their precollege educational experiences. Nevertheless, in the third chapter, we indicated that many of the programmatic initiatives implemented to help facilitate access to higher education for Black males are under attack due to budget restraints and litigious antiaffirmative action pursuits. Indeed, programs such as TRIO and college outreach programs (traditionally referred to as remedial education) are becoming increasingly endangered. As such, researchers must be more intentional about investigating functional partnerships between higher education and preK–12. Findings from such studies may provide the evidence needed to justify their existence in times of shrinking resources or reveal other avenues to promoting access such as summer bridge programs or compensatory experiences if TRIO-like efforts end (Strayhorn, 2013a). Doing this would help to preserve and strengthen access to higher education for Black men.

A sixth area of research that emerged from our review of literature is the need to continue to investigate ways to promote or increase campus engagement among Black males across all institutional types. In the third chapter, we emphasized a linkage between engagement on campus and a range of outcomes, such as increased academic and social integration and sense of belonging. Despite this, we know that engagement on campus for Black men is woefully low at institutions such as PWIs, HBCUs, and community colleges. While research has indicated that Black men enrolled in PWIs and community colleges have generally been less engaged on campus, this seems to be relatively new at HBCUs. For example, seminal research on Black students at HBCUs reported that Black men dominated the campuses of HBCUs and were actively involved in many leadership positions. Nevertheless, a study by Harper, Carini, Bridges, and Hayek (2004) revealed that gender gaps in campus engagement had narrowed over the years, as more women became engaged on campus, often assuming key leadership position previously held by men. While recent research has provided new and practical insight about ways to more effectively promote campus engagement for college students in general and Black men specifically (Harper & Quaye, 2009), it does not provide an in-depth treatment of Black men in diverse institutional contexts.

Finally, another area for further scholarly development is theory. As a whole, the experiences, perceptions, and outcomes of Black men have been undertheorized. Often, research on Black men has relied upon frameworks based on majority White student samples. While dominant theories may provide insight into Black male educational realities (as part of the greater student experience) they likely do not fully capture the intricacies, nuances, and unique sociocultural experiences of Black men. For example, using Tinto's (1993) integrationist theory, Wood (2012) and Strayhorn (2012b) examined the effect of academic and social integration on Black male persistence in the community colleges. Using data from two national data sets, Wood found that while academic integration was a positive predictor of persistence, social integration was a negative (albeit small) predictor of persistence. As such, the applicability of Tinto's model had smaller utility for understanding Black male success in community colleges than in four-year colleges and universities. This is merely one example of how traditional higher education canonical theory fails to address the distinctive realities of Black men. As a whole, the field of Black male studies in postsecondary education woefully lacks a standalone canon of theory beyond "cool pose" (Majors

& Billson, 1992), "African American male theory" (Bush & Bush, 2013), the anti-deficit achievement framework (Harper, 2010), and the African American male persistence model (Mason, 1998). New theories and models that address the specific experiential challenges and opportunities facing Black men are needed to undergird the next generation of research on these men.

Implications for Practice

In this section, we highlight five implications from our analysis and synthesis of the literature that might be helpful for educators and practitioners serving Black men in diverse postsecondary education contexts. First, the relationships that students have with faculty play an integral role in their retention and persistence. Despite this, research has firmly showed that Black men have encountered challenges to forming supportive relationships with faculty at PWIs and community colleges. At HBCUs, though it is well established that Black men have supportive relationships with faculty, some recent research has shown that Black men have unique challenges with faculty at these institutions (see Kimbrough & Harper, 2006; Palmer & Maramba, 2012), which warrants additional investigation. Clearly institutions—specifically PWIs and community colleges—need to be more proactive in ensuring that Black students encounter faculty who are supportive and student-centered. In order to help faculty achieve this goal, colleges and universities should mandate that faculty attend cultural awareness workshops to help them become more informed of how to work with students who differ from them racially, ethnically, and culturally. These workshops should take place on a frequent basis and their occurrence should be codified in institutional policy. Not only implementing these workshops, but also actively encouraging faculty, staff, and administrators to attend them, sends a strong message to the campus community that the institution values inclusiveness and wants to promote an environment where all students feel a sense of belonging.

In addition, institutions should also administer climate surveys to the campus community to have a better understanding of how various constituents of the campus community perceive the campus. If used appropriately, a survey of this nature could be useful to help the institution hold forums and other workshops about racial microaggressions and other issues that engender an uncomfortable campus climate in as well as outside the classroom for minority students in general and Black men specifically. Moreover, institutional administrators should also become familiar with the work of Hurtado, Milem, Clayton-Pedersen, and Allen (1999). In their research, they outline several steps that institutions could take to improve the campus climate for racial and ethnic minority students at PWIs. Furthermore, institutions should encourage faculty to be more intentional about establishing rapport and building critical relationships with students. One way to encourage relationship building between faculty and students is to provide opportunities for faculty and student to interact outside the classroom. Perhaps if faculty interacted more with students outside of class, they would get to know their students better, thus creating meaningful opportunities for faculty to debunk cultural stereotypes they may have about Black males and other college students.

Furthermore, research in the third chapter has shown the efficacy of mentorship on the retention and persistence of Black male college students. While research has indicated that Black males who attend HBCUs can readily find a mentor on campus (albeit some research has questioned this—see Kimbrough & Harper, 2006), research on Black students at PWIs has shown that outside of a few Black faculty and administrators on campus, Black males have challenges finding a mentor on campus. Though research has not thoroughly discussed Black male community college students' accessibility to mentors, given that they perceive faculty as unsupportive (though their relationships with administrators is not well understood), they may face similar challenges to finding a mentor on campus as their counterparts at PWIs. Nevertheless, colleges and universities should encourage and be proactive in linking Black men, particularly those who are first generation, up with a mentor. These mentors may be faculty, staff, administrators, alumni, or community members. College administrators should also be mindful that peer mentors can provide important guidance and support to Black men in postsecondary education. Black men, making the initial transition into college, may be able to relate more effectively to successful upperclassmen serving as peer mentors. Not only can peer mentors help to facilitate students' academic and social integration, but also they can share experiences of triumphs and struggles, and expose students to critical resources—academic and social—to help enrich the students' college experience. Aside from using mentors as a critical way to help increase the retention and persistence of Black men in higher education, institutions should also continue to establish Black Male Initiatives (BMIs). In reviewing literature in the third chapter, we observed that BMIs were implemented across all institutional types highlighted in this monograph. While BMIs play a significant role in helping to facilitate Black male success by helping them establish meaningful relationships with faculty, administrators, and peers, Wood and Palmer (2012) noted that many institutions with BMIs do not place emphasis on assessing the efficacy of these initiatives. Specifically, they discussed that assessment leads to improvement in core components and services of BMIs, which might enhance the effectiveness of these initiatives. Similar to Wood and Palmer, we recognize that merely having BMIs is not sufficient. In order to truly understand the value of these initiatives and their role in helping support the success of this student demographic, assessing BMIs should be a critical goal for institutions.

In addition to BMIs, researchers have generally regarded family support and involvement as an asset to the success of Black men in higher education (Barnett, 2004; Guiffrida, 2004; Palmer, Davis, & Maramba, 2011). Many institutions provide newsletters to parents and have family day. Although the Family Educational Rights and Privacy Act (FERPA) may limit the extent that institutions can actively engage family, institutions should think of more creative and innovative ways to form partnerships with parents in order to help maximize the holistic development and success of Black men. While it is clear that college administrators at PWIs and HBCUs actively try to establish some sort of connectedness with parents, to the extent that community colleges does this is unclear. Given that community colleges disproportionately serves a large number of nontraditional students, they may not feel that involving family in the college experience serves little to no practical value. However, if community colleges are not already proactive in partnering with families to help facilitate the success of Black males, perhaps they should try experimenting with this approach to gain greater insight into how it might impact Black male retention and persistence. Finding ways to involve families in campus programming and support might prove to be beneficial for the persistence and success of these students. Finally, institutions need to continue to provide programming to facilitate the gender identity development of Black men. Research has illustrated that a healthy gender identity serves as a critical linchpin to student development and academic success. From the literature examined, it is clear that some institutional types, such as PWIs are providing this type of programming; however, the extent that this is occurring at HBCUs and community colleges is less clear.

Implications for Policy

In light of the research overviewed in this monograph, this section delineates recommendations specific to state and federal policies that influence access and outcomes for Black men in postsecondary education. Here, we highlight several policies relevant to Black male success, they include: remediation (college readiness), financial aid, affirmative action, and TRIO programs.

As noted previously, remediation policies have been increasingly scrutinized due to a lack of understanding of what remediation is, who is being served, and the actual costs associated with remedial education (see Davis & Palmer, 2010). Given that prior research has shown that the elimination of remediation policies has a deleterious effect on Black male access to higher education (Kimbrough & Harper, 2006), we recommend that states allow four-year colleges and universities to maintain remedial course offerings. Admittedly, remediation is costly and can limit available resources for other academic programming. Policymakers may believe that students should have used available resources in preK–12 education to be prepared for college math, reading, and writing. With this viewpoint in mind, we offer a counterperspective.

As noted previously, Black male students (and students of color in general) are often concentrated in urban schools that lack quality teachers, have higher staff turnover rates, and have limited resources and funding (Cortese, 2007; Education Commission of the States, 2003; Humphrey et al., 2005; Rowland

& Coble, 2005). These circumstances present an uneven playing field for Black males, with an expectation that they will perform better than students in other schools despite the fact that the schools they attend have more structural challenges.

Following this line of thinking, college access is then more of a byproduct of the "neighborhood" a student was raised, rather than the quality and potential of the student. Remedial education serves as a pathway for equity in preparation, allowing students a short time frame (typically less than an academic year at a four-year) to transition into the full rigor of college academics. Students denied remedial offerings at a four-year institution will invariably enroll in community colleges and for-profit institutions, provided that they continue in their educational pursuits at all. Given that these institutions have lower attainment rates than public four-year and private not-for-profit four-year institutions (see the first chapter), remediation policies will serve as a filter for social stratification. For policymakers, this should be a concern given that stratification has economic implications for earning potential. As a result, decreased earnings can result in a more limited tax base and an overreliance on social services (Nevarez & Wood, 2010).

A second recommendation emanating from this monograph is the need for enhanced fiscal support for students attending college. The cost of attending a college or university has risen dramatically in recent years due to the economic recession which has further decreased state funding to postsecondary institutions. As a result, students are increasingly taking more loans to address the gap between the limits of grant funding and their total tuition, fees, and living expenses. We have employed extant research to argue that loans have a differential effect on college degree attainment for Black students (St. John, 2003; Wei & Carroll, 2004).

Even more concerning is the recent doubling of Stafford federally subsidized loan interest rates (up to 6.8%). Therefore, policymakers should consider addressing this issue. Though unproven due to its recent passage (and still to be determined implementation), the state of Oregon can serve as a case study for an aggressive policy-driven response to increasing tuition. The legislature unanimously approved a plan called "pay it forward, pay it back" which will allow students to attend a state community college or university tuition-free. After graduating, the cost of attendance will be paid back by the state directly appropriating 3% of their pay for 24 years (Kim, 2013). This is a particularly useful policy approach as it will benefit students who have been historically underrepresented and underserved in education while being a general plan that can aid all students.

Third, we recommend that policymakers continue to examine ways to support racially based programming. It is possible that affirmative action programs will be eliminated in the coming years. The national movement to undercut such programming has been widely successful (Jaschik, 2011) and even the recent court ruling in *Fisher* illustrates changing mindsets on the value, urgency, and utility of affirmative action among the Supreme Court justices (Barnes, 2013; Carr, 2013). As a result, policymakers should continue to support diverse student populations in being admitted to college while recognizing that the scope of the authorization to do so is eroding. Possibly, state-based approaches may yield more long-term results. For instance, while the Texas Top Ten plan was the focus of *Fisher*, the aspect of the plan that was called into question was how the remaining students (beyond the top 10%) were admitted to state institutions. However, the plan itself is an innovative approach to promoting diversity by focusing on regional contexts. In the plan, the top 10% of students from around the state (based on their respective schools) are automatically accepted for admittance into a state institution. Given the diversity of school demographics, this plan structuralizes opportunity by focusing in geographic diversity. While the plan is not without limitations, such as students transferring high schools to "game the system" and increase their class ranks, certain aspects of this plan may serve as a starting point for discourse on how to address enrollment opportunities that improve access rather than reduce it.

In response to national budget challenges, TRIO programs have experienced the effect of restricted funding. Sustained cuts have reduced the total number of students and range of support that TRIO programs can offer historically marginalized student groups (Bidwell, 2013; Burd, 2011). Furthermore, our experiential knowledge has illuminated the fact that TRIO programs (due to affirmative action rulings) may face increasing challenges in serving Black and Latino students, for whom TRIO programs such as the

Educational Opportunity Program (EOP) were originally intended. Many universities, in seeking to raise their rankings, have implemented more stringent admission guidelines. Often, EOP programs that have been afforded the ability to admit students on special admission policies have seen their student lines decrease or end. As such, policymakers at the federal level should advocate for increased funding to TRIO programs and require program officials to be more attentive to ensuring that those students most in need are in fact the individuals receiving services. Policymakers should consider providing additional monies (or prioritizing existing monies) for colleges and universities that allow programs such as EOP to share in admissions decision making.

Concluding Remarks

The purpose of this monograph has been to provide a synthesis and analysis of literature on Black men in postsecondary education. Specifically, this monograph sought to better examine and understand the experiences of Black men in diverse institutional types, such as PWIs, HBCUs, and community colleges. By synthesizing the literature on these men, we have overviewed the unique challenges they face in education as well as dispelled monolithic notions of a single Black male reality. Overall, we have illuminated both the current state of the literature (in preK–12 and postsecondary education) as well as provided guidance for future research, practice, and policy that can result in better outcomes for Black males in education.

Appendix

Presentations on Black Males at ASHE by Year

Note: This listing was constructed using title searches from the ASHE program. Presentations focused on Black men without being explicitly outlined in the title of the paper are not reflected.

2013 St. Louis

- Black Male Doctoral Student Socialization: A Mixed Methods Study and Critical Race Analysis (*General Conference—Paper*); Royel Johnson, Terrell L. Strayhorn, Michael S. Williams, Marjorie L. Dorime-Williams, Blossom, Barrett, and Karleton Munn.
- Negotiating Race and Sexual Orientation in the College Choice Process of Black Gay Males (*General Conference—Paper*); Dian Squire and Steve Mobley.
- Black Male Leaders: An Examination of Hegemonic Masculinity and Race Consciousness of University Presidents (*General Conference—Paper*); Jerry Whitmore.
- Transactional vs. Transformational Education: A Critical Race Theoretical Examination of Black Male Transfer Student Athletes' Experiences (*General Conference—Paper*); Joseph Cooper and Billy Hawkins.
- Morehouse College: Promoting Black Male Success in STEM (*General Conference—Paper*); Marybeth Gasman, Thai-Huy Nguyen, Clifton Conrad, Todd Carl Lundberg, and Felecia Commodore.

- (Re)Negotiating White Spaces: Understanding How Black College Men Negotiate Their Racial and Gendered Identities in Academic and Social Spaces (*General Conference—Roundtable*); Jonathan Berhanu.
- High-Achieving Black Male Experiences With Supportive Relationships During College Transition Programs: Implications for Retention (*General Conference—Poster*); Jarvis McCowin.
- The Spiritual Journeys and Spaces of Black Gay Male Undergraduate Students at Predominantly White Institutions (*General Conference—Poster*); Darris Means.
- Determinants of Intent to Transfer Among Black Male Community College Students: A Multinomial, Multi-Level Investigation of Student Engagement (*Council on Ethnic Participation—Paper*); J. Luke Wood and Robert T. Palmer.

2012 Las Vegas

- My Brother's Keeper: African American Male Mentor Relationships in Doctoral Programs (*General Conference—Roundtable*); Royel M. Johnson, Brandon Common, Michael Steven Williams, and Jerry Whitmore, Jr.
- The 'Scholar Pose' Paradox: Critical Perspectives on Expressions of Black Masculinity in the Academy (*General Conference—Roundtable*); Lorenzo Baber, Royel M. Johnson, Brandon Common, and Terrance Range.
- Black College Male Engagement and Identity: Researching Theory and Practice (*General Conference—Symposium*); Marco Barker, James Earl Davis, T. Elon Dancy, II, Fred Bonner, II, and Terrell L. Strayhorn.
- Black Male Faculty in Academe Speak: Contesting Hegemony Through Scholarly Personal Narrative (SPN) (*General Conference—Symposium*); Fred Bonner, II, T. Elon Dancy, II, Robert T. Palmer, J. Luke Wood, and Roland Mitchell.
- Black Males in Postsecondary Education: Examining Their Experiences in Diverse Institutional Contexts (*General Conference—Symposium*); J. Luke Wood, Chance Lewis, Jonathan Berhanu, Jerlando Jackson, Richard Reddick, Julian Vasquez-Heilig, Christopher Newman, and Marybeth Gasman.

- The Effect of Academic Variables on Persistence and Attainment Among Black Males in Community Colleges (*Council on Ethnic Participation—Roundtable*); J. Luke Wood.
- Black in the Rainbow? Findings on the Experiences of Black Gay Male Students at Historically Black Colleges and Universities (*Council on Ethnic Participation—Roundtable*); Darris Means.
- Counteracting Foreign Pedagogy With Cultural Inclusivity: Potential Impact of Culturally Inclusive Practices on Outcomes of Black Males in U.S. Postsecondary STEM Education (*Council on Ethnic Participation—Roundtable*); Raquel Rall.
- Quantifying the Socialization Process for Black Male Doctoral Students and Its Influence on Self-Efficacy (*Council on Ethnic Participation—Roundtable*); Terrell Strayhorn and Michael Williams.
- Complex Decisions: Exploring the College Choice Process for Black Gay Men as They Choose Between Historically Black Universities & Predominately White Institutions (*Council on Ethnic Participation—Roundtable*); Steve Mobley, Jr., and Dian Squire.
- Writing Their Own Stories of Success, When Failure for Them is NOT an Option: The Voices of Black Graduate and Professional College Men (*Council on Ethnic Participation—Poster*); Derrick Echoles.
- Critical Issues Facing Minority Men in Community College: Implications for Policy, Practice, and Future Research (*Council on Ethnic Participation—Symposium*); Frank Harris, III, J. Luke Wood, Victor Saenz, Eboni Zamani-Gallaher, Shaun Harper, Taryn Ozuna, Sarah Rodriguez, Jennifer Smith, and Luis Ponjuan. *Note:* This symposium included as two presentations focused on Black males.

2011 Charlotte

- In Search of Progressive Black Masculinities (*Council on Ethnic Participation—Paper*); Keon McGuire, Shaun Harper, and Jonathan Berhanu.
- The Same … but Different: Examining Background Characteristics Among Black Males in Public Two Year Colleges (*Council on Ethnic Participation—Paper*); J. Luke Wood.

- Deconstructing D'Augelli's Gay Identity Development Model and Its Applicability to Black Gay Male Undergraduates at Predominantly White Institutions (*General Conference—Roundtable*); James M. DeVita, Amanda M. Blakewood, and Terrell L. Strayhorn.
- Investigating Self-Efficacy and Persistence: Black Male Students' Experiences in a Black Male Leadership Program (*General Conference—Roundtable*); Marco Barker and Jared C. Avery.
- Uneven Playing Fields: Using Bourdieu's Social Field Theory to Examine the Experiences of Black Male Doctoral Students in Higher Education Programs (*General Conference—Roundtable*); Ferlin G. McGaskey, Adriel Hilton, and Ted N. Ingram.
- Leaving the Two-Year College: Predictors of Black Male Collegian Departure (*General Conference—Roundtable*); J. Luke Wood.
- High-Achieving African American Males in College: Navigating Historically Black College and University (HBCU) and Predominantly White (PWI) Context (*General Conference—Roundtable*); Fred Bonner, II.
- Academically Gifted Poor African American Males in STEM Disciplines (*General Conference—Paper*); Alonzo M. Flowers.
- The Other Curriculum: How Mass Media Can Shape Perceptions of College-Going for African American Males (*General Conference—Paper*); Ken Roth.
- Standing in the Intersection: African American, Male, Millennial College Students (*General Conference—Paper*); Fred Bonner, II, Alonzo M. Flowers, and Lonnie Booker.
- Black in the Rainbow? Preliminary Findings on the Experiences of Black Gay Male Students at Historically Black Colleges and Universities (*General Conference—Poster*); Darris Means and Audrey J. Jaeger.
- The Effects of Sexuality on the Self-Authorship of Gay Male College Students (*General Conference—Poster*); James L. Olive.

2010 Indianapolis

- A Qualitative Study of Masculinities and Gender Expression Among Black Men (*Paper*); Frank Harris and Robert T. Palmer.

- Gridiron and GPA: Academically Gifted African American Male Student Athletes in NCAA Division I-FBS Institutions (*Symposium*); John W. Murry, Fred A. Bonner, Mary Howard-Hamilton, Fitzgerald Hill, and Derrick Gragg.
- Quantifying Aspects of the Socialization Process for Black Male Doctoral Students and Measuring Its Influence on Satisfaction (*Roundtable*); Terrell L. Strayhorn.
- Family Matters: Facilitating the Academic Success of High Achieving African American Males in Predominately White Colleges and Universities (*Roundtable*); John W. Murry and Fred A Bonner, II.
- Creating Conditions of Mattering to Enhance Persistence for Black Males at an Historically Black University (*Roundtable*); Robert T. Palmer, Frank Harris, III, and Dina Maramba.

2009 Vancouver

- Manchild in the Promised Land: Selected Racial Factors and the Academic Achievement and College Aspirations of African American Males in an Urban High School (*Paper*); Larry Rowley, Christopher James Nellum, and Noe Ortega.
- Strategies for Success: Examining Social Capital Among African American Male Doctoral Students at Predominantly White Institutions (*Paper*); Ted Ingram and Adriel Hilton.
- The Emerging Scholar … the Forgotten African-American Male in College: A Demographic Study and Analysis With New Data and Lens (*Poster*); Ralph Hardin.

2008 Jacksonville

- Understanding Persistence Through the Voices of African American Men in Doctoral Programs at Predominantly White Institutions (*Paper*); Ted N. Ingram.

- Is It Really a "Man's World"? Reconsidering African American Men in Science, Technology, Engineering, and Mathematics at HBCUs (*Poster*); Valerie Lundy-Wagner.
- In Reflection: The Lived Experiences of Black Gay Men With an Undergraduate Degree From a Historically Black College or University (*Poster*); Obie Ford, III.
- The Vanishing African American and Latino Male in Higher Education: A Critical Dialogue at a Critical Time (*Symposium*); Victor Saenz, Luis Ponjuan, Julian Vasquez-Heilig, Richard J. Reddick, Sharon Fries-Britt, Mark A. Lopez, Wendell Diedrik Hall, Ana L. Romero, and Michael Cuyjet.
- The Impact of Family Support for African American Males at a Historically Black University: Affirming the Revision of Tinto's Theory (*Paper*); Robert T. Palmer and Ryan Davis.
- No African American Male Left Behind (*Poster*); John Hamilton.
- Factors Affecting the Success of African American Male Graduate Students in STEM and Education: A Sequential Mixed Methods Approach (*Paper*); Terrell Strayhorn and Michael Cuyjet.

2007 Louisville

- Determined to Succeed: The Impact of Non-Cognitive Variables on the Success of African American Men at Historically Black Universities (*Paper*); Robert T. Palmer and Terrell Strayhorn.
- African American Male Faculty Satisfaction: Does Institutional Type Make a Difference? (*Paper*); Kendricks Hooker and Barbara Johnson.
- How Black Male Students Experience the Politics of Historically Black Colleges and Universities (*Paper*); Shaun R. Harper and Marybeth Gasman.
- New Paradigms and New Promises: The First Generation African American Male Graduate Student (*Roundtable*); James Coaxum, III, and Jay Jones.

2006 Anaheim

- The Role of Summer Bridge Programs in Access, College Adjustment, and Persistence Among Black Male Undergraduates: Implications for Policy (*Paper*); Shaun R. Harper and Ryan J. Davis.

- Entering the Academy: Exploring the Socialization Experiences of African American Male Faculty (*Paper*); Dorian McCoy.
- From Challenge to Triumph: Examining Retention Strategies for African American Men in Doctoral Programs (*Roundtable*); Ted Ingram.

2005 Philadelphia

- Where Are All the African American Men? College Choice and the Black Male Enrollment Gap (*Roundtable*); Michael J. Smith.
- High-Achieving African American Men's Behavioral Responses to Stereotypes at Predominantly White Universities (*Paper*); Shaun R. Harper.
- 'The Pedestal Factor': Are We Setting Up Our African American Male Student-Athletes for Academic Success or Failure? (*Paper*); Athena Perrakis and Cheryl Getz.
- Persistence Factors Among College African American Males (*Paper*); James Coaxum and Ted Ingram.
- College Enrollment and the Socio-Cultural Capital Divide Between Young Black Men and Women (*Poster*); Kevin Eagan and Crystal Gafford.
- Understanding the Struggle: African American Men in Predominantly White and Historical Black Institutions in the South (*Paper*); T. Elon Dancy, II.

2004 Kansas City

- Towards Understanding the Social and Academic Integration of African American Males at Predominantly White Universities (*Poster*); T. Elon Dancy, II.
- Developing, Educating, and Mentoring African-American Men: Evaluating a Community-Based Effort to Increase African-American Male College Enrollment (*Poster*); Kijua Sanders-McMurtry.
- Voluntary Association Membership: Black Greek Men on a Predominantly White Campus (*Paper*); Stephanie M. McClure.

2003 Portland

- Home, School, and Community Factors That Influence African–American Males to Attend College (*Paper*); James Coaxum and Donavan D. Mc-Cargo.

References

Allen, W. R. (1992). The color of success: African American college students' outcomes at predominantly White and historically Black public colleges and universities. *Harvard Educational Review, 62*, 26–44.

Allen, W. R., & Jewell, J. O. (2002). A backward glance forward: Past, present and future perspectives on historically Black colleges and universities. *Review of Higher Education, 25*, 241–261.

Allen, W. R., Jewell, J. O., Griffin, K. A., & Wolf, D. S. (2007). Historically Black colleges and universities: Honoring the past, engaging the present, touching the future. *Journal of Negro Education, 76*(3), 263–280.

Alonzo, J., Tindal, G., & Robinson, Q. (2008). Using school wide response to intervention to close the achievement gap in reading. *Educational Research Service, 26*(1), 1–9.

Anderson, E. (2008). *Against the wall: Poor, young, Black, and male.* Philadelphia: University of Pennsylvania Press.

Anderson, J. (1988). *The education of Blacks in the South, 1860–1935.* Chapel Hill: The University of North Carolina Press.

Anyon, J. (1995). Race, social class, and educational reform in an inner-city school. *Teachers College Record, 97*, 69–94.

Aratani, Y., Wight, V. R., Cooper, J. L. (2011). *Racial gaps in early childhood: Socio-emotional health, developmental and educational outcomes among African American boys.* New York, NY: National Center for Children in Poverty. Retrieved from http://www.nccp.org/publications/pdf/text_1014.pdf

Aronson, J., Fried, C., & Good, C. (2002). Reducing the effects of stereotype threat on African American college students by shaping theories of intelligence. *Journal of Experimental Social Psychology, 38*, 113–125.

Asquith, C. (2007). Getting to know Dr. James T. Minor. *Diverse Issues in Higher Education, 23*(26), 10.

Astin, A. W. (1984). Student involvement: A developmental theory for higher education. *Journal of College Student Personnel, 25*, 297–308.

Astin, A. W. (1993). *What matters in college? Four critical years revisited.* San Francisco, CA: Jossey-Bass.

Attewell, P., Lavin, D., Domina, T., & Levey, T. (2006). New evidence on college remediation. *Journal of Higher Education, 77*, 886–924.

Aud, S., Fox, M., & Kewal Ramani, A. (2010). *Status and trends in the education of racial and ethnic groups (NCES 2010-015).* U.S. Department of Education, National Center for Education Statistics. Washington, DC: Government Printing Office.

Baggerly, J., & Max, P. (2005). Child-centered group play therapy with African American boys at the elementary school level. *Journal of Counseling and Development, 83*(4), 387–396.

Bahr, P. R. (2008). Does mathematics remediation work? A comparative analysis of academic attainment among community college students. *Research in Higher Education, 49*, 420–450.

Baker, B. D. (2001). Measuring the outcomes of state policies for gifted education: An equity analysis of Texas school districts. *Gifted Child Quarterly, 45*(2), 4–15.

Baldridge, B. J., Hill, M. L., & Davis, J. E. (2011). New possibilities: (Re)engaging Black male youth within community-based educational spaces. *Race, Ethnicity, and Education, 14*, 121–136.

Barnes, R. (2013, June 24). Supreme Court sends Texas affirmative action plan back for further review. *The Washington Post.* Retrieved from http://articles.washingtonpost .com/2013-06-24/politics/40157367_1_admissions-policies-grutter-justice-ruth-bader -ginsburg

Barnett, M. (2004). A qualitative analysis of family support and interaction among Black college students at an Ivy League University. *The Journal of Negro Education, 73*(1), 53–68.

Bennett, D. L., Lucchesi, A. R., & Vedder, R. K. (2010). *For-profit higher education: Growth, innovation and regulation.* Washington, DC: Center for College Affordability and Productivity. Retrieved from http://www.centerforcollegeaffordability.org /uploads/ForProfit_HigherEd.pdf

Bensimon, E. M. (2004). The diversity scorecard: A learning approach to institutional change. *Change, 36*(1), 45–52.

Bensimon, E. M. (2005). *Equality in fact, equality in results: A matter of institutional accountability.* Washington, DC: American Council on Education.

Bensimon, E. M. (2007). The underestimated significance of practitioner knowledge in the scholarship on student success. *The Review of Higher Education, 30*(4), 441–469.

Berger, J. B., & Milem, J. F. (1999). The role of student involvement and perceptions of integration in a causal model of student persistence. *Research in Higher Education, 40*(6), 641–664.

Berger, J. B., & Milem, J. F. (2000). Exploring the impact of historically Black colleges in promoting the development of undergraduates' self-concept. *Journal of College Student Development, 41*(4), 381–394.

Berhanu, J., & Jackson, J. F. L. (2012). Untold stories: An examination of selected experiences of Black male graduate students at an ivy league institution. In A. A. Hilton, J. L. Wood, & C. W. Lewis (Eds.), *Black males in postsecondary education: Examining their experiences in diverse institutional contexts* (pp. 49–74). Charlotte, NC: Information Age Publishing.

Bettinger, E. P., & Long, B. T. (2007). Remedial and developmental courses. In S. Dickert-Conlin & R. Rubenstein (Eds.), *Economic inequality and higher education: Access, persistence and success* (pp. 69–100). New York, NY: Russell Sage Foundation.

Bidwell, A. (2013). Sequestration presents uncertain outlook for students, researchers, and job-seekers. *The Chronicle of Higher Education.* Retrieved from http:// chronicle.com/article/Sequestration-Presents/137617/

Billie, N. M., & Carter, J. D. (2012). People, places, and things: Examining the impact of institutional characteristics on the experiences of Black males at a research intensive institution. In A. A. Hilton, J. L. Wood, & C. W. Lewis (Eds.), *Black males in postsecondary education: Examining their experiences in diverse institutional contexts* (pp. 125–150). Charlotte, NC: Information Age Publishing.

Billson, J. M. (1996). *Pathways to manhood: Young Black males struggle for identity*. New Brunswick, NJ: Transaction.

Bland, C. J., Meurer, L., & Maldonado, G. (1995). A systematic approach to conducting a nonstatistical meta-analysis of research literature. *Academic Medicine, 70*, 642–653.

Bledsoe, T., & Rome, K. (2006). Student African American brotherhood. In M. J. Cuyjet & Associates (Eds.), *African American men in college* (pp. 24–46). San Francisco, CA: Jossey-Bass.

Bond, H. M. (1935). The curriculum and the Negro child. *Journal of Negro Education, 4*(2), 159–168.

Bonner, F. A., II. (2010). *Academically gifted African American male college students*. Santa Barbara, CA: Praeger.

Bonner, F. A., II, & Bailey, K. W. (2006). Enhancing the academic climate for African American men. In M. J. Cuyjet & Associates (Eds.), *African American men in college* (pp. 24–46). San Francisco, CA: Jossey-Bass.

Bonous-Hammarth, M., & Boatsman, K. (1996, April). *Satisfaction guaranteed? Predicting academic and social outcomes for African Americans college students*. Paper presented at the annual conference of the American Educational Research Association, New York.

Boylan, H. R., & Bonham, B. S. (2007). 30 years of developmental education: A retrospective. *Journal of Developmental Education, 30*, 2–4.

Boylan, H. R., Bonham, B. S., & Tafari, G. N. (2005). Evaluating the outcomes of developmental education. In G. Gaither (Ed.), *New Directions for Institutional Research: No. 125. Minority retention: What works?* (pp. 59–72). San Francisco, CA: Jossey-Bass.

BPS. (2009a). *Beginning Postsecondary Students Longitudinal Study. First degree attained through 2009 by institutional sector level and control and (Black) and (male)*. Washington, DC: National Center for Education Statistics.

BPS. (2009b). *Beginning Postsecondary Students Longitudinal Study. Student degree intentions by institutional sector level and control and (Black) and (male)*. Washington, DC: National Center for Education Statistics.

Branch-Brioso, K. (2009). What will it take to increase Hispanics in STEM? Money, of course. *Diverse Education*. Retrieved from http://diverseeducation.com/article/12347/

Breneman, D. W., & Merisotis, J. P. (2002). Beyond money: Support strategies for disadvantaged students. In D. E. Heller (Ed.), *Conditions of access: Higher education for lower income students* (pp. 113–133). Westport, CT: Greenwood.

Brown, C. (2006). The impact of campus activities on African American college men. In M. J. Cuyjet & Associates (Eds.), *African American men in college* (pp. 47–67). San Francisco, CA: Jossey-Bass.

Brown, M. C. (1999a). Ebony men in the ivory tower: A policy perspective. In V. C. Polite & J. E. Davis (Eds.), *African American males in school and society: Practices and policies for effective education* (pp. 122–133). New York, NY: Teacher College Press.

Brown, M. C. (1999b). *The quest to define collegiate desegregation: Black Colleges, Title VI compliance, and post-Adams litigation.* Westport, CT: Bergin & Garvey.

Brown, M. C., & Dancy, T. E. (2008). An unsteady march toward equity: The political and educational contexts of African American educational attainment. In M. C. Brown & R. D. Bartee (Eds.), *The broken cisterns of African American education: Academic performance and achievement in the post-Brown era* (pp. 17–42). Charlotte, NC: Information Age Publishing.

Brown, M. C., Dancy, T. E., & Davis, J. E. (2007). Drowning beneath a rising tide: The common plight of public schools, disadvantaged students, and Black males. In S. P. Robinson & M. C. Brown II (Eds.), *The children Hurricane Katrina left behind: Schooling context, professional preparation, and community politics* (pp. 54–72). New York, NY: Peter Lang.

Brown, M. C., Dancy, T. E., & Davis, J. E. (2013). *Educating African American males: Contexts for consideration, possibilities for practice.* New York, NY: Peter Lang.

Brown, M. C., Dancy, T. E., & Norfles, N. (2007). A nation still at risk: No child left behind and the salvation of disadvantaged students. In F. Brown (Ed.), *No child left behind and other special programs in urban school districts* (pp. 341–364). Oxford, UK: Elsevier.

Brown v. Board of Education of Topeka, 347 U.S. 483 (1954).

Burd, S. (2011). Budgets cutters take aim at TRIO and Gear Up. *New America Foundation.* Retrieved from http://edmoney.newamerica.net/blogposts/2011/budget_cutters _take_aim_at_the_trio_and_gear_up_programs-49427

Bush, E. C., & Bush, L. (2004). Beware of false promises. *Community College Journal, 74*(5), 36–39.

Bush, E. C., & Bush, L. (2005). Black male achievement and the community college. *Black Issues in Higher Education, 22*(2), 44.

Bush, E. C., & Bush, L. (2010). Calling out the elephant: An examination of African American male achievement in community colleges. *Journal of African American Males in Education, 1*(1), 40–62.

Bush, L., & Bush, E. C. (2013). Introducing African American male theory (AAMT). *Journal of African American Males in Education, 4*(1), 6–17.

Callan, P. (2006, September). *Measuring up 2006: The national report card on higher education* (The National Center for Public Policy and Higher Education Report No. 06-5). San Jose, CA.

Campbell, D. B., & Fleming, J. (2000). Fear of success, racial identity, and academic achievement in black male college students. *Community Review, 18,* 5–18.

Canada, G. (1998). *Reaching up for manhood: Transforming the lives of boys in America.* Boston, MA: Beacon Press.

Carr, K. M. (2013, June 8). Supreme Court signals the end for affirmative action as we know it. *The Baltimore Sun.* Retrieved from http://articles.baltimoresun.com/2013-07-08 /news/bs-ed-affirmative-action-20130708_1_regents-v-affirmative-action-academic -freedom

Carter, R. (1996). The unending struggle for equal educational opportunity. In E. Lagemann & L. Miller (Eds.), *Brown v. Board of Education: The challenge for today's schools* (pp. 19–26). New York, NY: Teachers College Press.

Cashmore, E. (2004). *Encyclopedia of race and ethnic studies.* New York, NY: Routledge.

Chickering, A. W., & Reisser, L. (1993). *Education and identity.* San Francisco, CA: Jossey-Bass.

Chodorow, N. (1978). *The reproduction of mothering.* Berkeley: University of California.

Clement, R. (1966). The historical development of higher education for Negro Americans. *Journal of Negro Education, 35*(4), 299–305.

Coaxum, J., & McCargo, D. (2003, November). *Home, school, and community factors that influence African-American males to attend college.* Paper presented at the annual conference of the Association for the Study of Higher Education, Portland, OR.

Cokley, K. (2001). Gender differences among African American students in the impact of racial identity on academic psychosocial development. *Journal of College Student Development, 42,* 480–487.

Cokley, K. (2003). What do we know about the academic motivation of African American college students? Challenging the "anti-intellectual myth." *Harvard Educational Review, 73,* 524–558.

Coles, A. (1998). TRIO achievers: The promise of the future. *The Journal of Negro Education, 67,* 432–443.

Cooper, R., & Jordan, W. J. (2005). Cultural issues in comprehensive school reform. In O. S. Fashola (Ed.), *Educating African American males: Voices from the field* (pp. 1–18). Thousand Oakes, CA: Corwin Press.

Corbin, K., & Pruitt, R. (1999). Who am I? The development of the African American male identity. In V. Polite (Ed.), *African American males in school and society: Practices and policies for effective education* (pp. 68–81). New York, NY: Teacher College Press.

Cortese, A. (2007). *Here's the boost that poor children, their teachers, and their schools really need.* Retrieved from http://www.aft.org/newspubs/periodicals/ae/spring2007/cortese.cfm

Cose, E. (2003). *The envy of the world: On being a Black man in America.* New York, NY: Simon & Schuster.

Crenshaw, K. (1989). Demarginalizing the intersection of race and sex. *The University of Chicago Legal Forum, 140,* 139–167.

Cuyjet, M. J. (Ed.). (1997). *New Directions for Student Services: No. 80. Helping African American men succeed in college.* San Francisco, CA: Jossey-Bass.

Cuyjet, M. J. (2006). African American college men: Twenty-first century issues and concerns. In M. J. Cuyjet & Associates (Eds.), *African American men in college* (pp. 3–23). San Francisco, CA: Jossey-Bass.

Dancy, T. E. (2009). Black men on campus: What the media do not show us. *Diverse Issues in Higher Education, 25*(26), 21.

Dancy, T. E. (2010a). Faith in the unseen: The intersections of spirituality and identity among African American males in college. *Journal of Negro Education, 79*(3), 416–432.

Dancy, T. E. (2010b). *Managing diversity: (Re)visioning equity on college campuses.* New York, NY: Peter Lang.

Dancy, T. E. (2011). Colleges in the making of manhood and masculinity: Gendered perspectives on African American males. *Gender and Education, 23*(4), 477–495.

Dancy, T. E. (2012). *The brother code: Manhood and masculinity among African American men in college.* Charlotte, NC: Information Age Publishing.

Dancy, T. E. (in press). Theorizing manhood: Black male identity constructions in the education pipeline. In F. Bonner (Ed.), *Frameworks and models of black male success: A guide for P–12 and postsecondary educators.* Sterling, VA: Stylus.

Dancy, T. E., & Brown, M. C. (2008). Unintended consequences: African American male educational attainment and collegiate perceptions after Brown v. Board of Education. *American Behavioral Scientist, 51*(7), 984–1003.

Dancy, T. E., & Brown, M. C. (2012). *African American males and education: Researching the convergence of race and identity.* Charlotte, NC: Information Age Publishing.

Dancy, T. E., & Horsford, S. D. (2010). Considering the social context of school and campus communities: The importance of culturally proficient leadership. In S. D. Horsford (Ed.), *New perspectives in educational leadership: Exploring social, political, and community contexts and meaning* (pp. 153–171). New York, NY: Peter Lang.

Darensbourg, A., Perez, E., & Blake, J. J. (2010). Overrepresentation of African American males in exclusionary discipline: The role of school-based mental health professionals in dismantling the school to prison pipeline. *Journal of African American Males in Education, 1*(3), 196–211.

Darling-Hammond, L. (2005). New standards and old inequalities: School reform and the education of African American students. In J. E. King (Eds.), *Black education: A transformative research and action agenda for the new century* (pp. 197–223). Mahwah, NJ: Erlbaum.

Darling-Hammond, L. (2006). The flat earth and education: How America's commitment to equity will determine our future. *Educational Researcher, 36,* 318–334.

Davis, J. E. (1994). College in Black and White: Campus environment and academic achievement of African American males. *The Journal of Negro Education, 63,* 620–633.

Davis, J. E. (1999). What does gender have to do with the experiences of African American college men? In V. C. Polite & J. E. Davis (Eds.), *African American males in school and society: Practice and policies for effective education* (pp. 134–148). New York, NY: Teachers College Press.

Davis, J. E. (2000). Mothering for manhood: The (re)production of a Black son's gendered self. In M. C. Brown & J. E. Davis (Eds.), *Black sons to mothers: Compliments, critiques, and challenges for cultural workers in education* (pp. 51–67). New York, NY: Peter Lang.

Davis, J. E. (2001). Black boys in school: Negotiating masculinities and race. In R. Majors (Ed.), *Educating our Black children: New directions and radical approaches* (pp. 169–182). New York, NY: RoutledgeFalmer.

Davis, J. E. (2003). Early schooling and academic achievement of African American males. *Urban Education, 38*(5), 515–537.

Davis, J. E. (2012). Negotiating masculinity in college: African American males and academic engagement. In M. C. Brown, T. E. Dancy, & J. E. Davis (Eds.), *Educating African American males: Contexts for consideration, possibilities for practice* (pp. 53–66). New York, NY: Peter Lang.

Davis, R. J., & Palmer, R. T. (2010). The role and relevancy of postsecondary remediation for African American students: A review of research. *Journal of Negro Education, 79*(4), 503–520.

DeCuir, J. T., & Dixson, A. D. (2004). "So when it comes out, they aren't that surprised that it is there": Using critical race theory as a tool of analysis of race and racism in education. *Educational Researcher, 33*(5), 26–31.

DeSousa, J. (2001). Reexamining the educational pipeline for African Americans students. In L. Jones (Ed.), *Retaining African American in higher education: Challenges paradigms for retaining students, faculty and administrators* (pp. 21–44). Herndon, VA: Stylus.

Digest of Education Statistics. (2011a). *Higher Education General Information Survey (HEGIS), "Fall Enrollment in Colleges and Universities" surveys, 1976 and 1980; Integrated Postsecondary Education Data System (IPEDS), "Fall Enrollment Survey" (IPEDS-EF:90); and IPEDS*

Spring 2001 through Spring 2011, Enrollment component. Washington, DC: U.S. Department of Education, National Center for Education Statistics.

Digest of Education Statistics. (2011b). *Integrated Postsecondary Education Data System, "Fall Enrollment Survey" (IPEDS-EF:90); Spring 2001and Spring 2011, Enrollment component; Spring 2011, Finance component; and Fall 2010, Completions component.* Washington, DC: U.S. Department of Education, National Center for Education Statistics.

DiRamio, D., Ackerman, R., & Mitchell, R. L. (2008). From combat to campus: Voices of student-veterans. *NASPA Journal, 45*(1), 73–102.

Dobbie, W., & Fryar, R. G., Jr. (2011). *Getting beneath the veil of effective schools: Evidence from New York City.* Retrieved from http://www.nber.org/papers/w17632.pdf

DuBois, W. E. B. (1903). *The souls of Black folk.* Chicago, IL: A. C. McClurg.

Education Commission of the States. (2003). *Eight questions on teacher preparation: What does the research say? A summary of the findings.* Retrieved from http://www.ecs.org/html /educationissues/teachingquality/tpreport/home/summary.pdf

Educational Testing Service. (2011). *A strong start: Positioning young Black boys for educational success.* Retrieved from http://www.ets.org/s/sponsored_events/pdf/16818_BlackMale _trifold3_WEB.pdf

Ehrenberg, R. (1991). The demographic distribution of American doctorates. In C. Clotfelter, R. Ehrenberg, M. Getz, & J. Siegfried (Eds.), *Economic challenges in higher education* (pp. 211–232). Chicago, IL: University of Chicago Press.

Engs, R. F. (1999). *Educating the disenfranchised and the disinherited: Samuel Chapman Armstrong and Hampton institute, 1839–1893.* Knoxville: The University of Tennessee Press.

Esters, L. L., & Mosby, D. C. (2007). Disappearing acts: The vanishing Black male on community college campuses. *Diverse Issues in Higher Education, 24*(14), 45.

Fashola, O. S. (2003). Developing the talents of African American male students during non-school hours. *Urban Education, 38,* 398–430.

Feagin, J. R., Vera, H., & Imani, N. (1996). *The agony of education. Black students at White colleges and universities.* New York, NY: Nikitah Publications.

Fergus, E., & Noguera, P. (2010). *Theories of change among single-sex schools for Black and Latino boys: An intervention in search of theory.* New York: Metropolitan Center for Urban Education, New York University.

Ferguson, A. A. (2000). *Bad boys: Public schools in the making of black masculinity.* Ann Arbor: The University of Michigan.

Ferguson, A. A. (2007). Making a name for yourself: Transgressive acts and gender performance. In M. Kimmel & M. Messner (Eds.), *Men's lives* (7th ed., pp. 154–166). Boston, MA: Allyn and Beacon.

Ferguson, S. (2011). The utopian worldview of Afrocentricity: Critical comments on a reactionary philosophy. *Socialism and Democracy, 25*(1), 44–73.

Fisher v. University of Texas at Austin, 133 S. Ct. 2411 (2013).

Fleming, J. (1984). *Blacks in college: A comparative study of student success in Black and White institutions.* San Francisco, CA: Jossey-Bass.

Florida ex rel. Hawkins v. Board of Control of Florida, 350 U.S. 413 (1956).

Flowers, L. A. (2002). The impact of college racial composition on African American students' academic and social gains. Additional evidence. *Journal of College Student Development, 43*(3), 403–410.

Flowers, L. A. (2004). Examining the effects of student involvement on African American college student development. *Journal of College Student Development, 45*(6), 633–654.

Flowers, L. A. (2006). Effects of attending a 2-year institution on African American males' academic and social integration in the first year of college. *Teachers College Record, 108*(2), 267–286.

Foner, E. (1988). *Reconstruction: America's unfinished business, 1863–1877*. New York, NY: Harper & Row.

Fordham, S., & Ogbu, J. U. (1986). Black students' school success: Coping with the "burden of acting White." *The Urban Review, 18*(3), 179–205.

Fountaine, T. P. (2012). Examining the phenomenon of for-profit colleges and universities for minority students: Implications for Black males. In A. A. Hilton, J. L. Wood, & C. W. Lewis (Eds.), *Black males in postsecondary education: Examining their experiences in diverse institutional contexts* (pp. 29–48). Charlotte, NC: Information Age Publishing.

Freeman, T. L., & Huggans, M. A. (2009). Persistence of African-American male community college students in engineering. In H. T. Frierson, W. Pearson, Jr., & J. H. Wyche (Eds.), *Black American males in higher education: Diminishing, proportions* (pp. 229–252). Bingley, UK: Emerald Group.

Fries-Britt, S. L., & Turner, B. (2001). Facing stereotypes: A case study of Black students on a White campus. *Journal of College Student Development, 42*, 420–429.

Fries-Britt, S. L., & Turner, B. (2002). Uneven stories: Successful Black collegians at a Black and a White campus. *Review of Higher Education, 25*(3), 315–330.

Froomkin, D. (1998). *Affirmative action under attack*. Retrieved from http://acad .fcps.org/ss/puch/apps/readings/froomkin.pdf

Futrell, M. (1999). The challenge of the 21st century: Developing a highly qualified cadre of teachers to teach our nation's diverse student population. *Journal of Negro Education, 68*(3), 318–334.

Gardenhire-Crooks, A., Collado, H., Martin, K., & Castro, A. (2010). *Terms of engagement: Men of color discuss their experiences in community college*. New York, NY: MDRC.

Garibaldi, A. (1992). Educating and motivating African American males to succeed. *Journal of Negro Education, 61*(1), 4–11.

Gasman, M. (2008). Minority-serving institutions: An historical backdrop. In M. Gasman, B. Baez, & C. S. Turner (Eds.), *Understanding minority-serving institutions* (pp. 18–27). Albany, NY: SUNY Press.

Gasman, M. (2013). *The changing faces of historically Black colleges and universities*. Center for Minority Serving Institutions (MSIs). University of Pennsylvania Graduate School of Education. Retrieved from http://www.gse.upenn.edu/pdf/cmsi /Changing_Face_HBCUs.pdf

Gasman, M., Baez, B., Drezner, N. D., Sedgwick, K., Tudico, C., & Schmid, J. M. (2007). Historically Black colleges and universities: Recent trends. *Academe, 93*(1), 69–78.

Gasman, M., Lundy-Wagner, V., Ransom, T., & Bowman, N. (2010). *Unearthing promise and potential: Our nation's historically Black colleges and universities* [ASHE Higher Education Report, 35(5)]. San Francisco, CA: Jossey-Bass.

Gay, G., & Howard, T. C. (2001). Multicultural education for the 21st century. *Teacher Educator, 36*, 1–16.

Gordon, B. (2012). "Give a brotha a break!" The experiences and dilemmas of middle-class African American male students in white suburban schools. *Teachers College Record, 114*(4), 1–13. Retrieved from https://www.tcrecord.org/library/abstract.asp?contentid=16416

Green, A., & Glasson, G. (2009). African Americans majoring in science at predominantly White universities (A review of literature). *The College Student Journal, 43*, 366–374.

Greene, J., & Foster, G. (2003). *Public high school graduation and college readiness rates in the United States.* (Education Working Paper No. 3). New York, NY: Manhattan Institute, Center for Civic Information.

Grutter v. Bollinger, 539 U.S. 306 (2003).

Guiffrida, D. A. (2003). African American student organizations as agents of social integration. *Journal of College Student Development, 44*(3), 304–319.

Guiffrida, D. A. (2004). Friends from home: Asset and liability to African American students attending a predominantly White institution. *NASPA Journal, 24*(3), 693–708.

Guiffrida, D. A. (2005). Othermothering as a framework for understanding African American student definitions of student-centered faculty. *Journal of Higher Education, 76*(6), 701–723.

Gutman, L. M., & Schoon, I. (2013). *The impact of non-cognitive skills on outcomes for young people: Literature review* [Online]. London, UK: Education Endowment Foundation. Retrieved from http://educationendowmentfoundation.org.uk/uploads/pdf/Non-cognitive_skills_literature_review.pdf

Hagedorn, L. S., Maxwell, W., & Hampton, P. (2007). Correlates of retention for African American males in community colleges. In A. Seidman (Ed.), *Minority student retention: The best of the Journal of College Student Retention: Research, Theory, & Practice* (pp. 7–27). Amityville, NY: Baywood.

Hale, J. E. (2001). *Learning while Black: Creating educational excellence for African American children.* Baltimore, MD: The Johns Hopkins University Press.

Hall, C. W. (1973). *Black vocational technical and industrial arts education: Development and history.* Chicago, IL: American Technical Society.

Halpern, S. C. (1995). *On the limits of the law: The ironic legacy of Title VI of the 1964 Civil Rights Act.* Baltimore, MD: The Johns Hopkins University Press.

Hargrove, B. H., & Seay, S. E. (2011). School teacher perceptions of barriers that limit the participation of African American males in public school gifted programs. *Journal for the Education of the Gifted, 34*, 434–467.

Harper, P. B. (1996). *Are we not men? Masculine anxiety and the problem of African-American identity.* New York, NY: Oxford University Press.

Harper, S. R. (2004). The measure of a man: Conceptualizations of masculinity among high achieving African American male college students. *Berkeley Journal of Sociology, 48*(1), 89–107.

Harper, S. R. (2005). Leading the way: Inside the experiences of high-achieving African American male students. *About Campus, 10*(1), 8–15.

Harper, S. R. (2006a). *Black male students at public universities in the U.S.: Status, trends, and implications for policy, and practice.* Washington, DC: Joint Center for Political and Economic Studies.

Harper, S. R. (2006b). Peer support for African American male college achievement: Beyond internalized racism and the burden of "acting White." *Journal of Men's Studies, 14*(3), 337–358.

Harper, S. R. (2008). Realizing the intended outcomes of Brown: High-achieving African American male undergraduates and social capital. *American Behavioral Scientist, 51*(7), 1029–1052.

Harper, S. R. (2010). An anti-deficit achievement framework for research on students of color in STEM. In S. R. Harper & C. B. Newman (Eds.), *New Directions for Institutional Research: No. 148. Students of color in STEM* (pp. 63–74). San Francisco, CA: Jossey-Bass.

Harper, S. R. (2012). *Black male student success in higher education: A report from the National Black Male College Achievement Study.* Philadelphia: Center for Race and Equity in Education, University of Pennsylvania.

Harper, S. R. (2013). Am I my brother's teacher? Black undergraduates, peer pedagogies, and racial socialization in predominantly White postsecondary contexts. *Review of Research in Education, 37*(1), 183–211.

Harper, S. R., Carini, R. M., Bridges, K., & Hayek, J. C. (2004). Gender differences in student engagement among African American undergraduates at historically Black colleges and universities. *Journal of College Student Development, 45*(3), 271–284.

Harper, S. R., Davis, R. J., Jones, D. E., McGowan, B. L., Ingram, T. N., & Platt, C. S. (2011). Race and racism in the experiences of Black male resident assistants at predominantly White universities. *Journal of College Student Development, 52*(2), 180–200.

Harper, S. R., & Gasman, M. (2008). Consequences of conservatism: Black male undergraduates and the politics of historically Black colleges and universities. *Journal of Negro Education, 77*(4), 336–351.

Harper, S. R., & Griffin, K. A. (2011). Opportunity beyond affirmative action: How low-income and working class Black male achievers access highly selective, high-cost colleges and universities. *Harvard Journal of African American Public Policy, 17*(1), 43–60.

Harper, S. R., & Harris, F., III. (2006). The role of Black fraternities in the African American male undergraduate experience. In M. J. Cuyjet (Ed.), *African American men in college* (pp. 129–153). San Francisco, CA: Jossey-Bass.

Harper, S. R., & Harris, F., III. (2012). *Men of color: A role for policymakers in improving the status of Black male students in U.S. higher education.* Washington, DC: Institute for Higher Education Policy.

Harper, S. R., & Kuykendall, J. A. (2012). Institutional efforts to improve Black male student achievement: A standards-based approach. *Change, 44*(2), 23–29.

Harper, S. R., & Nichols, A. H. (2008). Are they not all the same? Racial heterogeneity among Black male undergraduates. *Journal of College Student Development, 49*(3), 1–16.

Harper, S. R., Patton, L. D., & Wooden, O. S. (2009). Access and equity for African American students in higher education: A critical race historical analysis of policy efforts. *Journal of Higher Education, 80,* 389–414.

Harper, S. R., & Quaye, S. J. (2007). Student organizations as venues for Black identity expression and development among African American male student leaders. *Journal of College Student Development, 48*(2), 127–144.

Harper, S. R., & Quaye, S. J. (Eds.). (2009). *Student engagement in higher education: Theoretical perspectives and practical approaches for diverse populations.* New York, NY: Routledge.

Harper, S. R., & Wood, J. L. (in press). *Advancing black male student success from preschool through Ph.D.* Sterling, VA: Stylus.

Harris, F. (1995). Psychosocial development and Black male masculinity: Implications for counseling economically disadvantaged African American male adolescents. *Journal of Counseling Development, 73*, 279–287.

Harris, F., III, & Harper, S. R. (2008). Masculinities go to community college: Understanding male identity socialization and gender role conflict. In J. Lester (Ed.), *New Directions for Community Colleges: No. 142. Gendered perspectives in community colleges* (pp. 25–35). San Francisco, CA: Jossey-Bass.

Harris, F., III, Palmer, R. T., & Struve, L. (2011). "Cool posing" on campus: A qualitative study of masculinities and gender expression among Black men at a private research institution. *Journal of Negro Education, 80*(1), 47–62.

Heller, D. E. (2003). *Informing public policy: Financial aid and student persistence.* Boulder, CO: Western Interstate Commission for Higher Education.

Henfield, M. S., Moore, J. L., III, & Wood, C. (2008). Inside and outside gifted education programming: Hidden challenges for African American students. *Exceptional Children, 74*, 433–450.

Herndon, M. K. (2003). Spirituality among African American college males. *Journal of Men's Studies, 12*, 75–84.

Herndon, M. K., & Hirt, J. B. (2004). Black students and their families: What leads to success in college. *Journal of Black Studies, 34*, 489–513.

Herrera, J. (1998). *The disproportionate placement of African Americans in special education: An analysis of ten cities* (Research Report No. UD032524). Washington, DC: U.S. Department of Education.

Higginbotham, A. L. (1996). *Shades of freedom: Racial politics and presumptions of the American legal process.* New York, NY: Oxford University Press.

Hilliard, A. G., III. (2000). Excellence in education versus high stakes standardized testing. *Journal of Teacher Education, 51*, 293–304.

Hilton, A. A., Wood, J. L., & Lewis, C. (Eds.). (2012). *Black males in postsecondary education: Examining their experiences in diverse institutional contexts.* Charlotte, NC: Information Age Publishing.

Hoffman, J., & Lowitzki, K. (2005). Predicting college success with high school grades and test scores: Limitations for minority students. *Review of Higher Education, 28*, 455–474.

Holzman, M. (2010). *Yes we can: The 2010 Schott 50 state report on public education and African American.* Cambridge, MA: Schott Foundation for Public Education.

hooks, b. (2004a). *The will to change: Men, masculinity, and love.* New York, NY: Atria Books.

hooks, b. (2004b). *We real cool: Black men and masculinity.* New York, NY: Routledge.

Hopkins, R. (1997). *Educating Black males: Critical lessons in schooling, community and power.* Albany, NY: The State University of New York Press.

Horn, C. L., & Flores, S. M. (2003). *The percentage plan in college admissions: A comparative analysis of the three states' experiences.* Cambridge, MA: The Civil Rights Project at Harvard University. Retrieved from http://civilrightsproject.ucla.edu/research/college-access/admissions/percent-plans-in-college-admissions-a-comparative-analysis-of-three-states2019-experiences/horn-percent-plans-2003.pdf

Howard, T. C. (2001). Powerful pedagogy for African American students: A case of four teachers. *Urban Education, 36*(2), 179–202.

Howard, T. C. (2003). A tug of war for our minds: African American high school students' perceptions of their academic identities and college aspirations. *High School Journal, 87*(1), 4–17.

Howard, T. C. (2010). *Why race and culture matters in schools: Closing the achievement gap in America's classrooms.* New York, NY: Teachers College Press.

Howard, T. C. (2013). How does it feel to be a problem? Black male students, schools, and learning in enhancing the knowledge base to disrupt deficit frameworks. *Review of Research in Education, 37*, 54–86.

Hrabowski, F., Maton, K. I., & Greif, G. L. (1998). *Beating the odds: Raising academically successful African American males.* New York, NY: Oxford University Press.

Humphrey, D. C., Koppich, J. E., & Hough, H. J. (2005). Sharing the wealth: National Board Certified Teachers and the students who need them most. *Education Policy Analysis Archives, 13*(18). Retrieved from http://epaa.asu.edu/ojs/article/view/123

Hunter, A., & Davis, J. E. (1992). Constructing gender: An exploration of Afro-American men's conceptualization of manhood. *Gender and Society, 6*(3), 464–479.

Hurtado, S., & Carter, D. F. (1997). Effects of college transition and perceptions of the campus racial climate on Latino students' sense of belonging. *Sociology of Education, 70*(4), 324–345.

Hurtado, S., Carter, D. F., & Spuler, A. (1996). Latino student transition to college: Assessing difficulties and factors in successful college adjustment. *Research in Higher Education, 37*(2), 135–157.

Hurtado, S., Milem, J., Clayton-Pedersen, A., & Allen, W. (1999). *Enacting diverse learning environments: Improving the climate for racial/ethnic diversity in higher education* [ASHE-ERIC Higher Education Report, *26*(8)]. Washington, DC: Graduate School of Education and Human Development, The George Washington University.

Ingram, T. N. (2013). Fighting F.A.I.R. (Feelings of Alienation, Isolation, and Racism): Using critical race theory to deconstruct the experiences of African American male doctoral students. *Journal of Progressive Policy and Practice, 1*(1), 1–18.

Integrated Postsecondary Education Data System (IPEDS). (2014). *Fall 2001 and Spring 2002 through Spring 2011, graduation rates component.* Washington, DC: U.S. Department of Education, National Center for Education Statistics.

Jackson, J. F. L. (2007). A systematic analysis of the African American educational pipeline to inform research, policy, and practice. In J. F. L. Jackson (Ed.), *Strengthening the educational pipelines for African Americans: Informing policy and practice* (pp. 1–14). New York: State University of New York Press.

Jackson, J. F. L., & Moore, J. L., III. (2006). African American males in education: Endangered or ignored. *Teachers College Record, 108*(2), 201–205.

Jackson, J. F. L., & Moore, J. L., III. (2008). The African American male crisis in education: A popular media infatuation or needed public policy response. *American Behavioral Science, 51*(7), 847–853.

Jaschik, S. (2011). *Throwing out a state vote.* Retrieved from http://www.insidehighered.com/news/2011/07/05/appeals_court_throws_out_michigan_ban_on_affirmative_action

Jenkins, T. (1958). Judicial discretion in desegregation: The Hawkins case. *Howard Law Journal, 4*, 193–203.

Joe, E. M., & Davis, J. E. (2010). Parental influence, school readiness and early academic achievement of African American boys. *Journal of Negro Education, 78*, 260–276.

Johnson, D. R., Soldner, M., Leonard, J. B., Alvarez, P., Inkelas, K. K., Rowan-Kenyon, H. T., & Longerbeam, S. D. (2007). Examining sense of belonging among first-year undergraduates from different racial/ethnic groups. *Journal of College Student Development, 48*(5), 525–542.

Jones, C. E., & Watt, J. D. (1999). Psychosocial development and moral orientation among traditional-aged college students. *Journal of College Student Development, 40*(2), 125–131.

Jones, L. (2002). *Making it on broke promises: Leading African American male scholars confront the culture of higher education.* Sterling, VA: Stylus.

Jordan, W., & Cooper, R. (2003). High school reform and Black male students: Limits and possibilities of policy and practice. *Urban Education, 38*, 196–216.

Kaltenbaugh, L. S., St. John, E. P., & Starkey, J. B. (1999). What differences does tuition make? An analysis of ethnic differences in persistence. *Journal of Student Financial Aid, 29*(2), 21–31.

Kaplin, W., & Lee, B. (2007). *The law of higher education.* San Francisco, CA: Jossey-Bass.

Kim, M., & Conrad, C. F. (2006). The impact of historically Black colleges and universities on the academic success of African American students. *Research in Higher Education, 47*, 399–427.

Kim, S. (2013, July 5). Oregon lawmakers pioneer tuition-free 'pay it forward, pay it back' college plan. *ABC News.* Retrieved from http://abcnews.go.com/Business/oregon-legislature-approves-tuition-free-college-pilot-program/story?id=19577994

Kimbrough, W. M. (1995). Self-assessment, participation, and value of leadership skills, activities, and experiences for Black students relative to their membership in historically Black fraternities and sororities. *Journal of Negro Education, 64*(1), 63–74.

Kimbrough, W. M. (1997). The membership intake movement of historically black Greek-letter organizations. *NASPA Journal, 34*, 229–239.

Kimbrough, W. M. (2003). *Black Greek 101: The culture, customs, and challenges of Black fraternities and sororities.* Madison, NJ: Fairleigh Dickinson University Press.

Kimbrough, W. M., & Harper, S. R. (2006). African American men at historically Black colleges and universities: Different environments, similar challenges. In M. J. Cuyjet (Ed.), *African American men in college* (pp. 189–209). San Francisco, CA: Jossey-Bass.

Kimbrough, W. M., & Hutcheson, P. A. (1998). The impact of membership in Black Greek-letter organizations on black students' involvement in collegiate activities and their development of leadership skills. *The Journal of Negro Education, 67*(2), 96–105.

Kimmel, M. (2000). *The gendered society.* New York, NY: Oxford University Press.

Kimmel, M. S., & Messner, M. A. (2007). *Men's lives* (7th ed.). New York, NY: Pearson.

Klopfenstein, K. (2004). Advanced placement: Do minorities have equal opportunity? *Economics of Education Review, 23*, 115–131.

Kluger, R. (1975). *Simple justice: The history of Brown v. Board of Education and Black America's struggle for equality.* New York, NY: Knopf.

Kober, N. (2001). *It takes more than testing: Closing the achievement gap. A report of the center on education policy.* Washington, DC: Center on Educational Policy.

Kuh, G. D. (2009). What student affairs professionals need to know about student engagement. *Journal of College Student Development, 50*(6), 683–706.

Kuh, G. D., & Hu, S. (2001). The effects of student faculty interaction in the 1990s. *Review of Higher Education, 24*(3), 309–332.

Kuh, G. D., Kinzie, J., Buckley, J., Bridges, B., & Hayek, J. C. (2007). *Piecing together the student success puzzle: Research, propositions, and recommendations* [ASHE Higher Education Report, *32*(5)]. San Francisco, CA: Jossey-Bass.

Kunjufu, J. (1986). *Countering the conspiracy to destroy Black boys.* Chicago, IL: Afro American Publishing.

Ladner, M. (2007). *Minority children and special education: Evidence of racial bias and strategies to avoid misdiagnosis. A briefing before the United States Commission on Civil Rights.* Washington, DC: Office of Civil Rights.

Ladson-Billings, G. (2011). Boyz to men? Teaching to restore Black boys' childhood. *Race, Ethnicity, and Education, 14,* 7–15.

Lagemann, E., & Miller, L. P. (Eds.). (1996). *Brown v. Board of Education: The challenge for today's schools.* New York, NY: Columbia University.

Landsman, J., & Lewis, C. (Eds.). (2006). *White teachers/diverse classrooms: A guide building inclusive schools, promoting high expectations, and eliminating racism.* Sterling, VA: Stylus.

LaVant, B., Anderson, J., & Tiggs, J. (1997). Retaining African American men through mentoring initiatives. In M. J. Cuyjet (Ed.), *New Directions for Student Services: No. 80. Helping African American men succeed in college* (pp. 43–53). San Francisco, CA: Jossey-Bass.

Lee, J. M. (2012). An examination of the participation of African American students in graduate education without public HBCUs. In R. T. Palmer, A. A. Hilton, & T. P. Fountaine (Eds.), *Black graduate education at historically Black colleges and universities* (pp. 61–82). Charlotte, NC: Information Age Publishing.

Legters, N. E., Balfanz, R., Jordan, W. J., & McPartland, J. M. (2004). Comprehensive reform for urban high schools. In J. H. Ballantine & J. Z. Spade (Eds.), *Schools and society: A sociological approach to education* (2nd ed., pp. 220–227). Belmont, CA: Thomson Wadsworth.

Levin, H. M., Belfield, C., Muennig, P., & Rouse, C. (2007). The public returns to public educational investments in African American males. *Economics of Educational Review, 26,* 700–709.

Levinson, M. (2007). *The civic achievement gap* (Circle Working Paper No. 51). College Park, MD: The Center for Information and Research on Civic Learning and Engagement.

Lewis, C. W., Butler, B. R., Bonner, F. A., II, & Joubert, M. (2010). African American male discipline patterns and school district responses resulting impact on academic achievement: Implications for urban educators and policy makers. *Journal of African American Males in Education, 1*(1), 7–25.

Lewis, C. W., & Erskine, K. F. (2008). *The dilemmas of being an African American male in the new millennium: Solutions for life transformation.* West Conshocken, PA: Infinity Publishing.

Lewis, C. W., & James, M. (2008). Framing African American students' success and failure in urban settings: A typology for change. *Urban Education, 43,* 127–153.

Lewis, S., Simon, C., Uzzell, R., Horwitz, A., & Casserly, M. (2010). *A call for change: The social and educational factors contributing to the outcomes of Black males in urban schools.* Washington, DC: The Council of the Great City Schools.

Libby, N. A. (2012). *Cracking down on PLUS loans.* Retrieved from http://www.insidehighered.com/news/2012/10/12/standards-tightening-federal-plus-loans

Losen, D., & Gillespie, J. (2012, August). *Opportunities suspended: The disparate impact of disciplinary exclusion from school.* Cambridge, MA: The Center for Civil Rights Remedies at the Civil Rights Project.

Losen, D., & Orfield, G. (2002). *Racial inequality in special education.* Cambridge, MA: Harvard Education Press.

Lott, J. (2011). Testing the factorial invariance of the Black racial identity scale across gender. *Journal of College Student Development, 52*(2), 224–234.

Love, P., & Talbot, D. (1999). Defining spiritual development: A missing consideration for student affairs. *Journal of Student Affairs Research and Practice, 37*(1), 361–375.

Lowe, E. Y. (1999). *Promise and dilemma: Perspectives on racial diversity and higher education.* Princeton, NJ: Princeton University Press.

Lum, L. (2009). The Obama era: A post-racial society? *Diverse: Issues in Higher Education, 25*(26), 14–16.

Lundberg, C. A., & Schreiner, L. A. (2004). Quality and frequency of faculty–student interaction as predictors of learning: An analysis by student race/ethnicity. *Journal of College Student Development, 45*(5), 549–565.

Lundy-Wagner, V. C., & Gasman, M. (2011). When gender issues are not just about women: Reconsidering Black men at historically Black colleges and universities. *Teachers College Record, 113*(5), 934–968.

Majors, R., & Billson, J. (1992). *Cool pose: The dilemmas of Black manhood in America.* New York, NY: Touchstone.

Majors, R., Tyler, R., Peden, B., & Hall, R. (1994). Cool pose: A symbolic mechanism for masculine role enactment and coping by Black males. In R. Majors & J. Gordon (Eds.), *The American Black male: His present status and future* (pp. 245–260). Chicago, IL: Nelson Hall.

Mandara, J. (2006). The impact of family functioning on African American males' academic achievement: A review and clarification of the empirical literature. *Teachers College Record, 108*(2), 206–223.

Marnie, S. (2002). *School finance: Per-pupil spending differences between selected inner city and suburban schools varied by metropolitan area.* Report to the Ranking Minority Member, Committee on Ways and Means, House of Representatives. Washington, DC: General Accounting Office.

Martin, B. E., & Harris, F. (2006). Examining productive conceptions of masculinities: Lessons learned from academically driven African American male student athletes. *The Journal of Men's Studies, 14*(3), 359–378.

Mason, H. P. (1994). *The relationships of academic, background, and environmental variables in the persistence of adult African American male students in an urban community college* (Doctoral dissertation). Available from ProQuest Dissertations and Theses database. (UMI No. 9430242)

Mason, H. P. (1998). A persistence model for African American male urban community college students. *Community College Journal of Research and Practice, 22*(8), 751–760.

Mattis, J. S. (2000). African American women's definitions of spirituality and religiosity. *Journal of Black Psychology, 26*(1), 101–122.

McClure, S. (2006). Exploring the meaning of membership: Black Greek men on predominantly White campuses. *Journal of Higher Education, 77*(6), 1036–1057.

McLaren, P. (2003). Critical pedagogy: A look at the major concepts. In A. Darder, M. Baltodano, & R. D. Torres (Eds.), *The critical pedagogy reader* (pp. 69–96). New York, NY: RoutledgeFalmer.

Merisotis, J. P., & Phipps, R. A. (2000). Remedial education in colleges and universities: What's really going on? *Review of Higher Education, 24*, 67–85.

Miller, D. K., & Mupinga, D. M. (2006). Similarities and differences between public and proprietary postsecondary 2-year technical institutions. *Community College Journal of Research and Practice, 30*, 565–577.

Milner, H. R. (2007). African American males in urban schools. No excuses—Teach and empower. *Theory into Practice, 46*, 239–246.

Minority Male Community College Collaborative. (n.d.). *Annotated bibliography on men of color in community colleges.* San Diego, CA: Interwork Institute, San Diego State University. Retrieved from http://interwork.sdsu.edu/sp/m2c3/resources-on-men-of-color/resources/

Missouri ex rel. Gaines v. Canada, 305 U.S. 337 (1938).

Mitchell, S. L., & Dell, D. M. (1992). The relationship between Black students racial identity, attitude, and participation in campus organizations. *Journal of College Student Developments, 33*(1), 39–43.

Moore, J. L. (2001). Developing academic warriors: Things that parents, administrators, and faculty should know. In L. Jones (Ed.), *In retaining African Americans in higher education: Challenging paradigms for retaining students, faculty, and administrators* (pp. 77–90). Herndon, VA: Stylus.

Moore, J. L., III, Henfield, M. S., & Owens, D. (2008). African American males in special education: Their attitudes and perceptions toward high school counselors and school counseling services. *American Behavioral Scientist, 51*, 907–927.

Moore, J. L., III, Madison-Colmore, O., & Smith, D. M. (2003). The prove them-wrong syndrome: Voices from unheard African-American males in engineering disciplines. *The Journal of Men's Studies, 12*, 61–73.

Mosby, J. R. (2009). *From strain to success: A phenomenological study of the personal and academic pressures on African American male community college students* (Doctoral dissertation). Retrieved from ProQuest Dissertations and Theses database. (UMI No. 3368203)

Mullin, C. M. (2010). *Just how similar? Community colleges and the for-profit sector* (Policy Brief 2010-04PBL). Washington, DC: American Association of Community Colleges.

Murrell, P. (1999). Responsive teaching for African American male adolescents. In V. C. Polite & J. E. Davis (Eds.), *African American males in school and society* (pp. 82–96). New York, NY: Teachers College Press.

Museus, S. D. (2008). Understanding the role of ethnic student organizations in facilitating cultural adjustment and membership among African American and Asian American college students. *Journal of College Student Development, 59*(6), 568–586.

Nasim, A., Roberts, A., Hamell, J. P., & Young, H. (2005). Non-cognitive predictors of academic achievement for African Americans across cultural contexts. *The Journal of Negro Education, 74*(4), 344–359.

National Center for Education Statistics. (2007). *Status and trends in the education of racial and ethnic minorities.* Washington, DC: Author.

National Center for Education Statistics. (2009). *National assessment of educational progress (NAEP), 2009 mathematics.* Washington, DC: Author.

National Center for Public Policy and Higher Education. (2011). *Policy alert: Affordability and transfer: Critical to increasing baccalaureate degree completion.* Retrieved from http://www.highereducation.org/reports/pa_at/index.shtml

National Collaborative on Diversity in the Teaching Force. (2004). *Assessment of diversity in America's teaching force: A call to action.* Retrieved from http://www.ate1.org/pubs/uploads/diversityreport.pdf

National Education Association. (2011). *Race against time: Educating Black boys.* Washington, DC: Author.

National Household Education Surveys (NHES). (2007). *Percentage of public school students in grades 6 through 12 who had ever been suspended by race/ethnicity and sex: 2007. Parent and Family Involvement in Education Survey of the National Household Education Surveys Program.* Washington, DC: U.S. Department of Education, National Center for Education Statistics.

National Postsecondary Student Aid Study (NPSAS). (2004). *Institution: sector by race/ethnicity for gender (male). 2003–04 National Postsecondary Student Aid Study (NPSAS:04).* Washington, DC: U.S. Department of Education, National Center for Education Statistics.

National Postsecondary Student Aid Study (NPSAS). (2012a). *NPSAS institution sector (4 with multiple) by race/ethnicity (with multiple) for gender (male).* Washington, DC: U.S. Department of Education, National Center for Education Statistics.

National Postsecondary Student Aid Study (NPSAS). (2012b). *NPSAS institution sector (4 with multiple) by dependency status, marital status, parents' highest education level, veteran status, types of dependents, average age as of 12/31/2011, average adjusted gross income (AGI).* Washington, DC: U.S. Department of Education, National Center for Education Statistics.

National Postsecondary Student Aid Study (NPSAS). (2012c). *Key elements dictionary: National Postsecondary Student Aid Study.* Washington, DC: U.S. Department of Education, National Center for Education Statistics.

Neal, L., McCray, A., Webb-Johnson, G., & Bridgest, S. (2003). The effects of African American movement styles on teachers' perceptions and reactions. *Journal of Special Education, 37,* 49–57.

Nevarez, C., & Wood, J. L. (2010). *Community college leadership and administration: Theory, practice and change.* New York, NY: Peter Lang.

Noguera, P. (2001, December). Joaquín's dilemma: Understanding the link between racial identity and school-related behaviors. *Motion Magazine.* Retrieved from http://www.inmotionmagazine.com/er/pnjoaq1.html

Noguera, P. (2008). *The trouble with Black boys: . . . and other reflections on race, equity and the future of public education.* San Francisco, CA: Jossey-Bass.

Noguera, P. (2012). Saving black and Latino boys: What schools can do to make a difference. *Phi Delta Kappan, 93*(5), 8–12.

Nora, A., & Cabrera, A. F. (1996). The role of perceptions in prejudice and discrimination and the adjustment of minority students to college. *Journal of Higher Education, 67,* 119–148.

Ogbu, J. U. (2003). *Black American students in an affluent suburb: A study of academic disengagement.* Mahwah, NJ: Lawrence Erlbaum.

Okech, A., & Harrington, R. (2002). The relationship between Black consciousness, self-esteem, and academic self-efficacy in African American men. *Journal of Psychology: Interdisciplinary and Applied, 136,* 214–224.

Omi, M., & Winant, H. (1989). *Racial formation in the United States: From the 1960s to the 1980s.* New York, NY: Routledge.

Osborne, J. (1997). Race and academic misidentification. *Journal of Educational Psychology, 89,* 728–735.

Outcalt, C. L., & Skewes-Cox, T. E. (2002). Involvement, interaction, and satisfaction: The human environment at HBCUs. *Review of Higher Education, 25*(3), 331–347.

Pace, C. R. (1990) *The undergraduates: A report of their activities and college experiences in the 1980s.* Los Angeles, CA: Center for the Study of Evaluation, UCLA Graduate School of Education.

Palmer, R. T. (2010). The perceived elimination of affirmative action and the strengthening of historically Black colleges and universities. *Journal of Black Studies, 40*, 762–776.

Palmer, R. T., & Davis, R. J. (2012). "Diamond in the Rough": The impact of a remedial program on college access and opportunity for Black males at an historically Black institution. *Journal of College Student Retention, 13*(4), 407–430.

Palmer, R. T., Davis, R. J., & Hilton, A. A. (2009). Exploring challenges that threaten to impede the academic success of academically underprepared African American male collegians at an HBCU. *Journal of College Student Development, 50*(4), 429–445.

Palmer, R. T., Davis, R. J., & Maramba, D. C. (2011). The impact of family support on the success of Black men at an historically Black university: Affirming the revision of Tinto's theory. *Journal of College Student Development, 52*(5), 577–593.

Palmer, R. T., Davis, R. J., Moore, J. L., III., & Hilton, A. (2010). A nation at risk: Increasing college participation and persistence among African American males to stimulate U.S. global competitiveness. *Journal of African American Males in Education, 1*(2), 105–124.

Palmer, R. T., & Gasman, M. (2008). "It takes a village to raise a child": The role of social capital in promoting academic success for African American men at a Black college. *Journal of College Student Development, 49*(1), 52–70.

Palmer, R. T., & Maramba, D. C. (2011). Using a tenet of critical theory to explain the African American male achievement disparity. *Education and Urban Society, 43*(4), 431–450.

Palmer, R. T., & Maramba, D. C. (2012). Creating conditions of mattering to enhance persistence for Black males at an historically Black university. *Spectrum: A Journal on Black Men, 1*(1), 95–120.

Palmer, R. T., & Maramba, D. C. (in press). A delineation of Asian American and Latino/a students' experiences with faculty at an historically Black college and university. *Journal of College Student Development.*

Palmer, R. T., Maramba, D. C., & Dancy, T. E. (2013). The magnificent "MILE": Impacting Black male retention and persistence at an HBCU. *Journal of College Student Retention, 15*(1), 65–72.

Palmer, R. T., Maramba, D. C., & Holmes, L. S. (2011). A contemporary examination of factors promoting the academic success of minority students at a predominantly White university. *Journal of College Student Retention, 13*(3), 329–348.

Palmer, R. T., & Strayhorn, T. L. (2008). Mastering one's own fate: Non-cognitive factors with the success of African American males at an HBCU. *National Association of Student Affairs Professionals Journal, 11*(1), 126–143.

Palmer, R. T., & Wood, J. L. (Eds.). (2012). *Black men in college: Implications for HBCUs and beyond.* New York, NY: Routledge.

Palmer, R. T., & Young, E. M. (2009). Determined to succeed: Salient factors that foster academic success for academically unprepared Black males at a Black college. *Journal of College Student Retention, 10*(4), 465–482.

Parker, M., & Flowers, L. A. (2003). The effects of racial identity on academic, achievement and perceptions of campus connectedness on African American students at predominantly White institutions. *College Student Affairs Journal, 22*(2), 180–194.

Parker, T. L. (2007). *Ending college remediation: Consequences for access and opportunity* (ASHE/Lumina Policy Briefs and Critical Essays No. 2). Ames: Department of Educational Leadership and Policy Studies, Iowa State University.

Pascarella, E. T., Edison, M., Nora, A., Hagedorn, L. S., & Terenzini, P. T. (1998). Does community college attendance influence students' educational plans? *Journal of College Student Development, 39*, 179–193.

Pascarella, E. T., & Terenzini, P. T. (2005). *How college affects students: A third decade of research* (Vol. 2). San Francisco, CA: Jossey-Bass.

Patterson, B. L., Thorne, S. E., Canam, C., & Jillings, C. (2001). *Meta-study of qualitative health research: A practical guide to meta-analysis and meta-synthesis.* Thousand Oaks, CA: Sage.

Patton, L. (2006). The voice of reason: A qualitative examination of Black student perceptions of Black cultural centers. *Journal of College Student Development, 47*(6), 628–646.

Perna, L. W. (2006). Understanding the relationship between information about college costs and financial aid and students' college related behaviors. *American Behavioral Scientist, 49*, 1620–1635.

Perrakis, A. I. (2008). Factor promoting academic success among African American and White male community college students. In J. Lester (Ed.), *New Directions for Community Colleges: No. 142. Gendered perspectives on community colleges* (pp. 15–23). San Francisco, CA: Jossey-Bass.

Plessy v. Ferguson, 163 U.S. 537 (1896).

Polite, V. C., & Davis, J. E. (1999). *African American males in school and society: Practices and policies for effective education.* New York, NY: Teachers College Press.

Poole, J. S. (2006). *Predictors of persistent Black male students' commitment to rural Mississippi two-year public institutions* (Doctoral dissertation). Available from ProQuest Dissertations and Theses database. (UMI No. 3211245)

Porter, K., & Soper, S. (2003, Spring). *Closing the achievement gap: Urban schools.* Comprehensive School Reform Connection. Washington, DC: National Clearinghouse for Comprehensive School Reform.

Prakash, M. S., & Waks, L. J. (1985). Four conceptions of excellence. *Teachers College Record, 87*(1), 79–101.

Preer, J. L. (1982). *Lawyers v. educators: Black colleges and desegregation in public higher education.* Westport, CT: Greenwood.

Price, J. N. (2000). *Against the odds: The meaning of school and relationships in the lives of six African American men.* Greenwich, CT: Ablex.

Prince, H., & Choitz, V. (2012, April). The public return to increasing postsecondary credential attainment. *CLASP.* Retrieved from http://www.clasp.org/resources-and-publications/publication-1/Full-Paper-The-Credential-Differential.pdf

Reid, K. (2013). Understanding the relationship among racial identity, self-efficacy, institutional integration and academic achievement of Black males attending research universities. *The Journal of Negro Education, 82*(1), 75–93.

Reid, M. J., & Moore, J. L. (2008). College readiness and academic preparation for postsecondary education: Oral histories of first-generation urban college students. *Urban Education, 43*, 240–261.

Reynolds, R. (2010). "They think you're lazy," and other messages Black parents send their Black sons: An exploration of critical race theory in the examination of educational outcomes of Black males. *Journal of African American Males in Education, 1*(1), 143–165.

Rideaux, L. (2004). *African American male participation at Tomball College: Barriers, outreach, and retention* (Doctoral dissertation). Available from ProQuest Dissertations and Theses database. (UMI No. 3150598)

Riegg, C. S. (2006). *The economics of two-year college education: Essays on community colleges and proprietary schools* (Unpublished doctoral dissertation). University of California, Los Angeles.

Rios, V. (2011). *Punished: Policing the lives of Black and Latino boys*. New York: New York University Press.

Rist, R. (1970). Student social class and teacher expectations: The self-fulfilling prophecy in ghetto education. *Harvard Educational Review, 40*, 411–451.

Robinson, S., Stempel, A., & McCree, I. (2005). *Gaining traction, gaining ground: How some high schools accelerate learning for struggling students* (Rep.). Washington, DC: The Education Trust.

Roderick, M. (2003). What's happening to the boys? Early high school experiences and school outcomes among African American male adolescents in Chicago. *Urban Education, 38*, 538–607.

Roebuck, J. B., & Murty, K. S. (1993). *Historically Black colleges and universities: Their place in American higher education*. Westport, CT: Praeger.

Rong, X. L. (1996). Effects of race and gender on teachers' perceptions of the social behavior of elementary students. *Urban Education, 31*, 261–290.

Rooks, N. M. (2013). For Black students, college degrees are separate and unequal. *The Chronicle of Higher Education*. Retrieved from http://chronicle.com/blogs/conversation/2013/07/10/for-black-students-college-degrees-are-separate-and-unequal/

Rosas, M., & Hamrick, F. A. (2002). Postsecondary enrollment and academic decision making: Family influences on women college students of Mexican descent. *Equity & Excellence in Education, 35*(1), 59–69.

Rosenthal, R., & Jacobson, L. (1968). *Pygmalion effect in the classroom: Teacher expectations and pupils intellectual development*. New York, NY: Holt, Rhinehart, & Watson.

Ross, M. (1998). *Success factors of young African American males at a historically Black college*. Westport, CT: Bergin and Garvey.

Ross, R. E. (2012). *A counter to the proposed crisis: Exploring the experiences of successful African American males* (Doctoral dissertation). University of Colorado, Denver, CO.

Rowland, C., & Coble, C. (2005, November). *Targeting teacher retention and recruitment policies for at-risk schools*. Napierville, IL: Learning Point Associates/North Central Regional Educational Laboratory.

Sax, L. J., Bryant, A. N., & Harper, C. E. (2005). The differential effects of student–faculty interaction on college outcomes for women and men. *Journal of College Student Development, 46*(6), 642–659.

Schlossberg, N. K. (1989). Marginality and mattering: Key issues in building community. In D. C. Roberts (Ed.), *Designing campus activities to foster a sense of community* (pp. 5–15). San Francisco, CA: Jossey-Bass.

Schott Foundation for Public Education. (2012). *The urgency of now: The Schott 50 state report on public education and Black males.* Retrieved from http://www.blackboysreport.org

Schott Foundation for Public Education. (2013). *A rotting apple: Education redlining in New York City.* Retrieved from http://schottfoundation.org/publications-reports/education-redlining

Scott, J. A. (2012). "Reaching out to my brothers": Improving the retention of low-income Black men at historically Black colleges and universities: A critical review of the literature. In R. T. Palmer & J. L. Wood (Eds.), *Black men in college: Implications for HBCUs and beyond* (pp. 57–70). New York, NY: Routledge.

Sewell, T. (1997, March). *Teacher attitude: Who's afraid of the big Black boys?* Paper presented at the Annual Meeting of the American Educational Research Association, Chicago, IL.

Sissoko, M., & Shiau, L. (2005). Minority enrollment demand for higher education at historically Black colleges and universities from 1976 to 1998: An empirical analysis. *The Journal of Higher Education, 76,* 181–208.

Smedley, B. D., Myers, H. F., & Harrell, S. P. (1993). Minority-status stresses and the college adjustment of ethnic minority freshmen. *Journal of Higher Education, 64*(4), 434–452.

Smith, W. A., Allen, W. R., & Danley, L. L. (2007). "Assume the Position ... You Fit the Description": Campus racial climate and the psychoeducational experiences and racial battle fatigue among African American male college students. *American Behavioral Scientist, 51*(4), 551–578.

Snyder, T. D., & Dillow, S. A. (2012). *Digest of education statistics 2011 (NCES 2012-001).* Washington, DC: National Center for Education Statistics, Institute of Education Sciences, U.S. Department of Education.

Spatig-Amerikaner, A. (2012, August). *Unequal education federal loophole enables lower spending on students of color.* Center for American Progress. Retrieved from http://www.americanprogress.org/wp-content/uploads/2012/08/UnequalEduation.pdf

Spivey, D. (1978). *Schooling for the new slavery: Black industrial education, 1868–1915.* Westport, CT: Greenwood Press.

Steele, C. M. (1992). Race and the schooling of Black Americans. *Atlantic Monthly, 269,* 68–78.

Steele, C. M. (1997). A threat in the air: How stereotypes shape intellectual identity and performance. *American Psychologist, 52,* 613–629.

Stefkovich, J., & Leas, T. (1994). A legal history of desegregation in higher education. *Journal of Negro Education, 63*(3), 406–420.

Steinberg, L., Dornbusch, S. M., & Brown, B. B. (1992). Ethnic differences in adolescent achievement: An ecological perspective. *American Psychologist, 45,* 347–355.

Stevens, C. D. (2006). *Skating the zones: African-American male students at a predominantly White community college* (Unpublished doctoral dissertation). New York University, New York.

Stinson, D. W. (2006). African American male adolescents, schooling (and mathematics): Deficiency, rejection, and achievement. *Review of Educational Research, 76,* 477–506.

St. John, E. P. (2002). *The access challenge: Rethinking the causes of the new inequality* (Policy Issues Report). Bloomington: Education Policy Center, Indiana University.

St. John, E. P. (2003). *Refinancing the college dream: Access, equal opportunity, and justice for taxpayers*. Baltimore, MD: John Hopkins University Press.

St. John, E. P., Hu, S., & Weber, J. (2001). State policy and the affordability of public higher education: The influence of state grants on persistence in Indiana. *Research in Higher Education, 42*(4), 401–428.

St. John, E. P., Paulsen, M. B., & Starkey, J. B. (1996). The nexus between college choice and persistence. *Research in Higher Education, 37*(2), 175–220.

St. John, E. P., & Starkey, J. B. (1995). An alternative to net price: Assessing the influence of prices and subsidies on within-year persistence. *Journal of Higher Education, 66*(2), 156–186.

Stone, D. (1997). *Policy paradox: The art of political decision making*. New York, NY: W. W. Norton.

Strayhorn, T. L. (2006). Factors influencing the academic achievement of first-generation college students. *Journal of Student Affairs Research and Practice, 43*(4), 1278–1307.

Strayhorn, T. L. (2008a). The role of supportive relationships in facilitating African American males' success in college. *NASPA Journal, 45*(1), 26–48.

Strayhorn, T. L. (2008b, May 12). Teacher expectations and urban Black males' success in school: Implications for academic leaders. *Academic Leadership, 16*(2). Retrieved from http://contentcat.fhsu.edu/cdm/compoundobject/collection/p15732coll4/id/261

Strayhorn, T. L. (2008c). Fittin' in: Do diverse interactions with peers affect sense of belonging for Black men at predominantly White institutions? *NASPA Journal, 45*(4), 501–527.

Strayhorn, T. L. (2009). Different hopes, different folks, the educational aspirations of African American males in urban, suburban, and rural high schools. *Urban Education, 44*(6), 710–731.

Strayhorn, T. L. (2010). When race and gender collide: Social and cultural capital's influence on the academic achievement of African American and Latino males. *Review of Higher Education, 33*(3), 307–332.

Strayhorn, T. L. (2011). Traits, commitments, and college satisfaction among Black American community college students community college. *Journal of Research and Practice, 35*(6), 437–453.

Strayhorn, T. L. (2012a). *College students' sense of belonging: A key to educational success*. New York, NY: Routledge.

Strayhorn, T. L. (2012b). Satisfaction and retention among African American men at two-year community colleges. *Community College Journal of Research and Practice, 36*(5), 358–375.

Strayhorn, T. L. (2013a). Academic achievement: A higher education perspective. In J. Hattie & E. Anderman (Eds.), *International guide to student achievement* (pp. 16–18). New York, NY: Routledge.

Strayhorn, T. L. (Ed.). (2013b). *Living at the intersections: Social identities and Black collegians*. Charlotte, NC: Information Age Publishing.

Strayhorn, T. L. (2013c). What role does grit play in the academic success of Black male collegians at predominately White institutions. *Journal of African American Studies*. Retrieved from http://cherp.ehe.osu.edu/files/2012/02/Strayhorn2013WhatRoleDoesGritPlay.pdf

Strayhorn, T. L., & DeVita, J. M. (2010). African American males' student engagement: A comparison of good practices by institutional type. *Journal of African American Studies, 14,* 87–105.

Strong American Schools. (2008). *Diploma to nowhere.* Washington, DC: Author.

Sutton, E. M. (2006). Developmental mentoring of African American college men. In M. J. Cuyjet & Associates (Eds.), *African American men in college* (pp. 95–111). San Francisco, CA: Jossey-Bass.

Sutton, E. M., & Kimbrough, W. M. (2001). Trends in Black student involvement. *NASPA Journal, 39*(1), 30–40.

Swail, W. S., Redd, K. E., & Perna, L. W. (2003). *Retaining minority students in higher education: A framework for success* [ASHE-ERIC Higher Education Report, 30(2)]. San Francisco, CA: Jossey-Bass.

Talbert-Johnson, C. (2004). Structural inequities and the achievement gap in urban schools. *Education and Urban Society, 37,* 22–36.

Taylor, C. M., & Howard-Hamilton, M. F. (1995). Student involvement and racial identity attitudes among African American males. *Journal of College Student Development, 36,* 330–336.

Taylor, R. (1989). Black youth, role models, and the social construction of identity. In R. Jones (Ed.), *Black adolescents* (pp. 155–171). Berkley, CA: Cobb & Henry.

Terry, C. L. (2010). Prisons, pipelines, and the President: Developing critical math literacy through participatory action research. *Journal of African American Males in Education, 1*(2), 73–104.

Thomas, E. P., Farrow, E. V., & Martinez, J. (1998). A TRIO Program's impact on participant graduation rates: The Rutger's University student support services program and its network of services. *Journal of Negro Education, 67,* 389–403.

Tienda, M., Niu, S., & Cortes, K. E. (2006). College selectivity and the Texas top 10% law: How constrained are the options? *Economics of Education Review, 25,* 259–272.

Tinto, V. (1993). *Leaving college: Rethinking the causes and cures of student attrition* (2nd ed.). Chicago, IL: The University of Chicago Press.

Titus, M. A. (2006). Understanding the influence of the financial context of institutions on student persistence at four-year colleges and universities, *Journal of Higher Education, 77*(2), 353–375.

Toldson, I. (2008). *Breaking barriers: Plotting the path to academic success for school-age African American males.* Washington, DC: Congressional Black Caucus Foundation.

Toldson, I., Harrison, M., Perine, R., Carreiro, P. & Caldwell, D. (2006). Assessing the impact of family process on rural African American adolescents' competence and behavior using latent growth curve analysis. *Journal of Negro Education, 75,* 440–442.

Tracey, T. J., & Sedlacek, W. E. (1985). The relationship of noncognitive variables to academic success: A longitudinal comparison by race. *Journal of College Student Personnel, 26,* 405–410.

Trent, W. T., Owens-Nicholson, D., Eatman, T. K., Burke, M., Daughtery, J., & Kathy, N. (2003). Justice, equality of educational opportunity and affirmative action in higher education. In M. Chang, D. Witt, J. Jones, & K. Hakuta (Eds.), *Compelling interest examining the evidence on racial dynamics in higher education* (pp. 22–48). Stanford, CA: Stanford Education.

Turner, C. S. V., González, J. C., & Wood, J. L. (2008). Faculty of color in academe: What 20 years of literature tells us. *Journal of Diversity in Higher Education, 1*(3), 139–168.

University of California Regents v. Bakke, 438 U.S. 265 (1978).

U.S. Census Bureau. (2000). *Projections of the resident population by age, sex, race, and hispanic origin: 1999 to 2100.* Washington, DC: Author.

U.S. Census Bureau. (2011). *CPS 2011 annual social and economic supplement.* Retrieved from http://www.census.gov/prod/techdoc/cps/cpsmar11.pdf

U.S. Census Bureau. (2012). *The 2012 statistical abstract: The national data book. Table 233: Mean earnings by highest degree earned (2009).* Washington, DC: U.S. Department of Commerce, Census Bureau.

U.S. Department of Commerce, Census Bureau, American Community Survey. (2007–2009). *Bureau of Justice Statistics, Prison inmates at Midyear, Current Population Survey.* Washington, DC: Author.

U.S. Department of Education, The National Commission on Excellence in Education. (1983). *A nation at risk: The imperative for educational reform.* Washington, DC: Author.

U.S. Government Accountability Office (U.S. GAO). (1995). *Higher education: Restructuring student aid could reduce low-income student dropout rate* (GAO/HEHS-95-48). Washington, DC: U.S. Government Printing Office.

U.S. Government Accountability Office (U.S. GAO). (2011). *Postsecondary education: Student outcomes vary at for-profit, nonprofit, and public schools* (GAO-12-143). Washington, DC: Author. Retrieved from http://www.gao.gov/assets/590/586738.pdf

Vernez, G., & Mizell, L. (2001). *GOAL: To double the rate of Hispanics earning a bachelor's degree.* Santa Monica, CA: RAND.

Wagner, A. (2006, September). *Measuring up internationally: Developing skills and knowledge for the global knowledge economy* (Report No. 06-7). San Jose, CA: The National Center for Public Policy and Higher Education.

Wagener, U., & Nettles, M. (1998). It takes a community to educate students. *Change, 30*(2), 18–25.

Wainrib, B. R. (1992). *Gender issues across the lifecycle.* New York, NY: Springer.

Watson, L. (2006). How does spirituality and religious activity affect the African American male college experience. In M. J. Cuyjet & Associates (Eds.), *African American men in college* (pp. 112–127). San Francisco, CA: Jossey-Bass.

Weddle-West, K., Hagan, W. H., & Norwood, K. M. (2013). Impact of college environments on the spiritual development of African American students. *Journal of College Student Development, 54*(3), 299–314.

Wei, C. C., & Carroll, C. D. (2004). *A decade of undergraduate student aid: 1989–90 to 1999–2000.* Washington, DC: National Center for Education Statistics.

Weiner, L. (2000). Research in the '90s: Implications for urban teacher preparation. *Review of Educational Research, 70*, 369–406.

Williams, T. R., Davis, L. E., Saunders, J., & Williams, J. H. (2002). Friends, family, and neighborhood: Understanding academic outcomes of African American youth. *Urban Education, 37*, 408–431.

Williams, Z. T. (2012). Dreams from my father: President Barack Obama and the reconstruction of African American men's history and studies—A response to the Ford Foundation Report, *Why we can't wait.* In T. E. Dancy & M. C. Brown (Eds.), *African American males and education: Researching the convergence of race and identity* (pp. 29–56). Charlotte, NC: Information Age Publishing.

Winbush, R. A. (2001). *The warrior method: A program for rearing health Black boys.* New York, NY: Amistad.

Wolters, R. (1984). *The burden of Brown: Thirty years of school desegregation.* Knoxville, TN: University of Tennessee Press.

Wood, J. L. (2008). Ethical dilemmas in African-American faculty representation. *Journal of Education Policy.* Retrieved from http://jlukewood.com/wp-content/uploads/2009/12/Ethical-Dilemmas-in-African-American-Faculty-Representation.pdf

Wood, J. L. (2011, August 5). Laying the groundwork—Black male programs and initiatives in community colleges. *Community College Times.* Retrieved from http://www.ccdaily.com/Pages/Opinions/Developing-successful-black-male-programs-and-initiatives.aspx

Wood, J. L. (2012). Leaving the two-year college: Predictors of Black male collegian departure. *Journal of Black Studies, 43*(3), 303–326.

Wood, J. L. (2013). The same...but different: Examining background characteristics among Black males in public two year colleges. *Journal of Negro Education, 82*(1), 47–61.

Wood, J. L., & Essien-Wood, I. R. (2012). Capital identity projection: Understanding the psychosocial effects of capitalism on Black male community college students. *Journal of Economic Psychology, 33*(3), 984–995.

Wood, J. L., & Harris, F., III. (2013). The community college survey of men: An initial validation of the instrument's non-cognitive outcomes construct. *Community College Journal of Research and Practice, 37,* 333–338.

Wood, J. L., & Hilton, A. A. (2012a). Community colleges—A metasynthesis of literature on Black males: An overview of 40 years of policy recommendations. In A. A. Hilton, J. L. Wood., & C. W. Lewis (Eds.), *Black males in postsecondary education: Examining their experiences in diverse institutional contexts* (pp. 5–28). Charlotte, NC: Information Age Publishing.

Wood, J. L., & Hilton, A. A. (2012b). Spirituality and academic success: Perceptions of African American males in community college. *Religion & Education, 39*(1), 28–47.

Wood, J. L., & Hilton, A. A. (2013). Moral choices: Towards a conceptual model of Black male moral development (BMMD). *Western Journal of Black Studies, 37*(1), 14–27.

Wood, J. L., Hilton, A. A., & Lewis, C. (2011). Black male collegians in public two-year colleges: Student perspectives on the effect of employment on academic success. *National Association of Student Affairs Professionals Journal, 14*(1), 97–110.

Wood, J. L., & Palmer, R. T. (2012). Innovative initiatives and recommendations for practice and future research: Enhancing the status of Black men at HBCUs and beyond. In R. T. Palmer & J. L. Wood (Eds.), *Black men in college. Implications for HBCUs and beyond* (pp. 176–196). New York, NY: Routledge.

Wood, J. L., & Palmer, R. T. (2013). Understanding the personal goals of Black male community college students: Facilitating academic and psychosocial development. *Journal of African American Studies, 17,* 222–241.

Wood, J. L., & Palmer, R. T. (in press). Academic achievement and the community college: Perspectives of Black male students on the importance of 'Focus.' *College Student Affairs Journal.*

Wood, J. L., & Turner, C. S. V. (2011). Black males and the community college: Student perspectives on faculty and academic success. *Community College Journal of Research & Practice, 35*, 135–151.

Wood, J. L., & Vasquez Urias, M. (2012). Community college vs. proprietary school outcomes: Student satisfaction among minority males. *Community College Enterprise, 18*(2), 83–100.

Wood, J. L., & Williams, R. C. (2013). Persistence factors for Black males in community college: An examination of background, academic, social, and environmental variables. *Spectrum: A Journal on Black Men, 1*(2), 1–28.

Wright, R. (1945/2005). *Black boy*. New York, NY: HarperCollins.

Name Index

Good, C., 42
Gordon, B., 44
Green, A., 77
Greene, J., 59
Greif, G. L., 28, 80, 81, 82
Griffin, K. A., 11, 58
Guiffrida, D. A., 63, 68, 70, 79, 95
Gutman, L. M., 80

H
Hagan, W. H., 79
Hagedorn, L. S., 16, 65, 66, 77
Hale, J. E., 43
Hall, C. W., 31
Hall, R., 83
Halpern, S. C., 31
Hamell, J. P., 81
Hampton, P., 16, 65, 66
Hamrick, F. A., 79
Hargrove, B. H., 42
Harper, C. E., 70
Harper, P. B., 49
Harper, S. R., 4, 6, 8, 12, 20, 55, 56, 58,
    59, 60, 61, 62, 63, 64, 67, 68, 69, 70,
    71, 73, 74, 75, 82, 83, 84, 90, 92, 93,
    94, 96
Harrell, S. P., 63
Harrington, R., 81
Harris, F., 46, 47, 49, 73, 74, 80, 82, 83,
    84
Harrison, M., 43
Hayek, J. C., 77, 92
Heller, D. E., 76
Henfield, M. S., 27, 37
Herndon, M. K., 44, 78
Herrera, J., 10
Hill, M. L., 45
Hilliard, A. G., III, 42
Hilton, A. A., 2, 4, 6, 7, 9, 11, 13, 20, 27,
    61, 65, 66, 76, 78, 83, 89
Hirt, J. B., 44
Hoffman, J., 56
Holmes, L. S., 72
Holzman, M., 28
hooks, b., 41, 50
Horn, C. L., 58

Horsford, S. D., 38
Horwitz, A., 9
Hough, H. J., 9, 96
Howard, T. C., 27, 28, 36, 37, 38, 41, 42,
    43, 44, 45, 46, 51
Howard-Hamilton, M. F., 72, 82
Hrabowski, F., 28, 80, 81, 82
Hu, S., 70, 76
Huggans, M. A., 17
Humphrey, D. C., 9, 96
Hunter, A., 50
Hurtado, S., 63, 68, 79, 94
Hutcheson, P. A., 73

I
Imani, N., 63, 70, 71
Ingram, T. N., 8, 63, 64
Inkelas, K. K., 68

J
Jackson, J. F. L., 7, 12, 29, 30, 31, 55, 83
Jacobson, L., 41
James, M., 43
Jaschik, S., 58, 98
Jenkins, T., 33
Jewell, J. O., 11, 23
Jillings, C., 6
Joe, E. M., 44
Johnson, D. R., 68
Jones, C. E., 67
Jones, D. E., 63, 64
Jones, L., 42
Jordan, W. J., 39, 43, 43, 88, 89
Joubert, M., 9

K
Kaltenbaugh, L. S., 77
Kaplin, W., 57
Kathy, N., 42
Kewal Ramani, A., 36
Kim, M., 60, 61
Kim, S., 98
Kimbrough, W. M., 59, 60, 61, 62, 69, 70,
    72, 73, 90, 93, 94, 96
Kimmel, M., 42, 84
Kinzie, J., 77

Subject Index

A

Academic success: and campus engagement, 67–76; in postsecondary education, 76–84
Advanced Placement (AP) classes, 39–40
After-school programs, 45
ASHE. *See* Association for the Study of Higher Education (ASHE)
Association for the Study of Higher Education (ASHE), 2, 4; conference presentations on Black males, 3, 101–108

B

Bad Boys: Public Schools in the Making of Black Masculinity, 47
BGLFs. *See* Black Greek Letter Fraternities (BGLFs)
Black Greek Letter Fraternities (BGLFs), 72–73
Black Male Initiatives (BMIs), 74
Black male population: access to higher education for, 56–60; at community colleges, 64–67; in degree-granting institutions, 13; experiences of, 1–5; at HBCUs, 60–63; future research on, implications for, 87–93; policy on, implications for, 96–99; practice, implications for, 93–96; peer-reviewed studies on, 1–5; in postsecondary

education, 11–24, 53–56, 76–84; in preK–12 education, 7–11; at PWIs, 63–64; in society and education, 1–5; in U.S. schools, 34–51
Black Men in College: Implications for HBCUs and Beyond, 90
BMIs. *See* Black Male Initiatives (BMIs)
Brown vs. Board of Education of Topeka, 32

C

Campus engagement, 67–76; benefits of, 68; Black Greek Letter Fraternities and, 72–73; Black Male Initiatives and, 74; faculty–student interaction in, 70; mentors role in, 75–76; outcomes of, 67–68; peer interaction, influences of, 71–72; student organizations and, 68–69
CCSEQ. *See* Community College Student Experiences Questionnaire (CCSEQ)
Center for Civil Rights Remedies, 36
Challenge Journal: A Journal of Research on African American Men, 1
College readiness programs, 58–60
College Student Experience Questionnaire (CSEQ), 67
Community-based organizations, 45
Community College Journal of Research and Practice, 4
Community colleges, Black males at, 64–67; faculty interaction in, 66;

premature departure from, 65; success in, 65–66

Community College Student Experiences Questionnaire (CCSEQ), 66

"Confrontational voice," 49

"Cool pose," 49–50

CSEQ. *See* College Student Experience Questionnaire (CSEQ)

E

Educational pipeline, Black males in, 30–33; Brown ruling and, 32–33; school desegregation in, 31–32; Slave Codes and, 30; "new slavery," 30–31

The Envy of the World: On Being a Black Man in America, 46

F

Faculty–student interaction, 70

Family Educational Rights and Privacy Act (FERPA), 95

FERPA. *See* Family Educational Rights and Privacy Act (FERPA)

Fisher vs. University of Texas, 58

Florida ex rel. Hawkins vs. Board of Control of Florida suit, 33

G

GAO. *See* General Accounting Office (GAO)

General Accounting Office (GAO), 14, 76–77

Gifted and Talented programs, 39–40

Grutter vs. Bollinger, 58

H

HBCUs. *See* Historically Black college and universities (HBCUs)

Historically Black college and universities (HBCUs), 7, 23; Black males at, 60–63; degrees awarded by, 22–23; enrollment in, 15–16

I

Integrated Postsecondary Education Data System (IPEDS), 65

IPEDS. *See* Integrated Postsecondary Education Data System (IPEDS)

J

Journal of African American Males in Education (JAAME), 1

Journal of African American Men, 1

Journal of African American Studies, 1

Journal of Black Masculinity, 1

M

Male gender role conflict (MGRC), 83, 84

MGRC. *See* Male gender role conflict (MGRC)

Missouri ex rel. Gaines vs. Canada, 31

N

NAEP. *See* National Association of Educational Progress (NAEP)

NASPA, 2

National Association of Educational Progress (NAEP), 37

NPSAS, 17

O

OECD. *See* Organisation of Economic Cooperation and Development (OECD)

Organisation of Economic Cooperation and Development (OECD), 27

P

Parent PLUS loan (PPL), 77

Peer interaction, 70–72

Plessy vs. Ferguson, 31

Postsecondary education, Black males in, 11–24, 55–85; access to, 55–60; and affirmative action, 57–58; and campus engagement, 67–76; characteristics of, 16–20; college and university enrollment of, 12–16; at community colleges, 64–67; educational outcomes, 20–25; enrollment in HBCUs, 16, 60–63; family support, 79–80; financial stability, 19; financial support, 76–78; masculine identity, 82–84;

non-cognitive factors for success, 80–81; at PWIs, 63–64; racial identity, 81–82; and remedial programs, 58–60; scholarship on, 5–7; spirituality, 78–79; success in, 22, 55–60, 76–84; and TRIO programs, 56–57
PPL. *See* Parent PLUS loan (PPL)
Predominantly White Institutions (PWIs), 7; Black males at, 63–64; academic environment of, 63–64; faculty members at, 63
PreK–12 education, Black males in, 7–11; exclusionary discipline in, 9–11; placement in special education, 10; stereotypical messages, 8–9
PWIs. *See* Predominantly White institutions (PWIs)

R
Remedial programs, 58–60
Rotting Apple: Education Redlining in New York City, A, 39

S
Schott Foundation for Public Education, 31–40
Schott Foundation Report, 35, 36, 37
Slave Codes, 30
SLD. *See* Students labeled disabled (SLD)

Souls of Black Folk, The, 40
Spectrum: A Journal of Black Men, 1
Student-centered learning, 38
Student engagement. *See* Campus engagement
Student organizations, 68–70

T
TRIO programs, 56–57

U
University of California Regents vs. Bakke, 57
U.S. schools, Black males in, 33–51; in Advanced Placement classes, 39–40; background, family, and community factors, 43–44; boyhood, masculinity, and identity factors, 46–51; and common core standards, 37; community-based organizations, role of, 45; discipline policies, 36; in Gifted and Talented programs, 39–40; graduation rates of, 34–35; "lockout crisis," 36; parental involvement and, 43; "pushout crisis," 35–36; in special education, 37–38; "snow days," effect on, 35; student-centered learning in, 38; success factors in, 44–46; teacher perceptions of, 41–43

About the Authors

Robert T. Palmer, PhD, is an active researcher and associate professor of student affairs at the State University of New York at Binghamton. He earned his PhD in higher education administration from Morgan State University in 2007, MS in counseling with an emphasis on higher education at West Chester University of Pennsylvania in 2003, and BS in history at Shippensburg University of Pennsylvania in 2001. His research examines issues of access, equity, retention, persistence, and the college experience of racial and ethnic minorities, particularly Black men as well as other student groups at historically Black colleges and universities (HBCUs). Since completing his PhD, his work has been published in national refereed journals, and he has authored/coauthored well more than 85 academic publications, including refereed journal articles, book chapters, and other academic publications. In 2009, the American College Personnel Association's (ACPA) Standing Committee for Men recognized his excellent research on Black men with its Outstanding Research Award. In 2011, he was named an ACPA Emerging Scholar and in 2012, he received the Carlos J. Vallejo Award of Emerging Scholarship from the American Education Research Association (AERA). Furthermore in 2012, he was awarded the Association for the Study of Higher Education (ASHE)-Mildred García Junior Exemplary Scholarship Award. Most recently, he was recognized as an Outstanding Reviewer by AERA.

J. Luke Wood, PhD, is an associate professor of administration, rehabilitation, and postsecondary education at San Diego State University. He teaches courses on evaluation and quantitative research in the doctoral program in community college leadership. He is codirector of the Minority Male Community College Collaborative (M2C3), a national project that partners with community colleges across the United States to enhance success among men of color. He is also the editor of the *Journal of African American Males in Education (JAAME)*, chair of the Multicultural & Multiethnic Education (MME) special interest group of the American Educational Research Association (AERA), and chair-elect for the Council on Ethnic Participation (CEP) for the Association for the Study of Higher Education (ASHE). His research focuses on factors impacting the success of Black (and other minority) male students in the community college. In particular, his research examines contributors to positive outcomes (e.g., persistence, achievement, attainment, and transfer) for these men. He has authored nearly 70 publications, including almost 40 peer-reviewed journal articles. His scholarship and professional practice have been lauded through awards and honors, including the Council for the Study of the Community College *Barbara K. Townsend Emerging Scholar Award*; the National Association for Student Personnel Administrator's *Newly Published Research Award* from the Knowledge Community on Men and Masculinities; and the ASHE Council on Ethnic Participation *Mildred Garcia Award for Exemplary Scholarship*.

T. Elon Dancy II, PhD, is an associate professor of higher education at The University of Oklahoma in Norman. He holds joint appointments in African & African American Studies, Women's & Gender Studies, and the Center for Social Justice. His research agenda investigates the experiences and sociocognitive outcomes of college students, particularly related to the nexus of race, gender, and culture. More specifically, his research informs the scholarly literature and institutional practices incident to African-American males in K–20 educational settings. With more than 50 publications to his credit, he is the author/editor of four books: *Managing Diversity: (Re)Visioning Equity on College Campuses, The Brother Code: Manhood and Masculinity Among African American Men in College, Educating African American Males: The Challenges of Context and the Possibilities for Practice*, and *African American Males and Education: Researching the Convergence of Race and Identity*. Additionally, he has received funding for his work related to males of color and STEM achievement from the National Science Foundation. His honors and awards include the 2005 Association for the Study of Higher Education-Council on Ethnic Participation Emerging Scholar Award and the 2008 American Educational Research Association Citation for Dissertation Excellence in Postsecondary Education. He was twice named an Emerging Education Policy Scholar from both the Thomas B. Fordham and American Enterprise Institutes. In 2014, *Diverse Issues in Higher Education* named him Top-Emerging Scholar.

Terrell L. Strayhorn, PhD, is an associate professor of higher education in the Department of Educational Studies, College of Education and Human Ecology at The Ohio State University, where he also serves as director of the Center for Inclusion, Diversity, & Academic Success (IDEAS), faculty research associate in the Kirwan Institute for the Study of Race & Ethnicity, senior research associate in the Todd Bell National Resource Center for African American Males, and faculty affiliate in the Departments of African and African American Studies, Engineering Education, and Sexuality Studies. He maintains an active and highly visible research agenda focusing on major policy issues in education: student access and achievement, equity and diversity, impact of college on students, and student learning and development. Acclaimed higher education researcher and policy analyst, he has authored seven books and monographs including *The Evolving Challenges of Black College Students* (Stylus Publishing) and *College Students' Sense of Belonging* (Routledge), more than 40 book chapters, and more than 80 refereed journal articles, reviews, and scientific reports. Named "one of the most highly visible new scholars in his field," by the *Journal of Blacks in Higher Education*, he has received numerous national awards and honors, and recently *Diverse Issues in Higher Education* named him one of the nation's Top-Emerging Scholars. Grants totaling more than $2 million have supported his research program including funds from the U.S. Department of Education, National Science Foundation, and several professional associations. He is also associate editor of the *Journal of Higher Education*, *NASAP Journal*, and coeditor of *Spectrum: A Journal on Black Men.*

About the ASHE Higher Education Report Series

Since 1983, the ASHE (formerly ASHE-ERIC) Higher Education Report Series has been providing researchers, scholars, and practitioners with timely and substantive information on the critical issues facing higher education. Each monograph presents a definitive analysis of a higher education problem or issue, based on a thorough synthesis of significant literature and institutional experiences. Topics range from planning to diversity and multiculturalism, to performance indicators, to curricular innovations. The mission of the Series is to link the best of higher education research and practice to inform decision making and policy. The reports connect conventional wisdom with research and are designed to help busy individuals keep up with the higher education literature. Authors are scholars and practitioners in the academic community. Each report includes an executive summary, review of the pertinent literature, descriptions of effective educational practices, and a summary of key issues to keep in mind to improve educational policies and practice.

The Series is one of the most peer reviewed in higher education. A National Advisory Board made up of ASHE members reviews proposals. A National Review Board of ASHE scholars and practitioners reviews completed manuscripts. Six monographs are published each year and they are approximately 144 pages in length. The reports are widely disseminated through Jossey-Bass and John Wiley & Sons, and they are available online to subscribing institutions through Wiley Online Library (http://wileyonlinelibrary.com).

Call for Proposals

The ASHE Higher Education Report Series is actively looking for proposals. We encourage you to contact one of the editors, Dr. Kelly Ward (kaward@wsu.edu) or Dr. Lisa Wolf-Wendel (lwolf@ku.edu), with your ideas.

Recent Titles

ASHE HIGHER EDUCATION REPORT

ORDER FORM SUBSCRIPTION AND SINGLE ISSUES

DISCOUNTED BACK ISSUES:

Use this form to receive 20% off all back issues of *ASHE Higher Education Report*.
All single issues priced at **$23.20** (normally $29.00)

TITLE   ISSUE NO.   ISBN

_____   _____   _____
_____   _____   _____
_____   _____   _____

*Call 888-378-2537 or see mailing instructions below. When calling, mention the promotional code JBNND
to receive your discount. For a complete list of issues, please visit www.josseybass.com/go/aehe*

SUBSCRIPTIONS: (1 YEAR, 6 ISSUES)

☐ New Order   ☐ Renewal

U.S.	☐ Individual: $174	☐ Institutional: $327
CANADA/MEXICO	☐ Individual: $174	☐ Institutional: $387
ALL OTHERS	☐ Individual: $210	☐ Institutional: $438

*Call 888-378-2537 or see mailing and pricing instructions below.
Online subscriptions are available at www.onlinelibrary.wiley.com*

ORDER TOTALS:

Issue / Subscription Amount: $ _____

Shipping Amount: $ _____
(for single issues only – subscription prices include shipping)

Total Amount: $ _____

SHIPPING CHARGES:

First Item $6.00
Each Add'l Item $2.00

*(No sales tax for U.S. subscriptions. Canadian residents, add GST for subscription orders. Individual rate subscriptions must
be paid by personal check or credit card. Individual rate subscriptions may not be resold as library copies.)*

BILLING & SHIPPING INFORMATION:

☐ **PAYMENT ENCLOSED:** *(U.S. check or money order only. All payments must be in U.S. dollars.)*

☐ **CREDIT CARD:**   ☐ VISA   ☐ MC   ☐ AMEX

   Card number _____Exp. Date_____

   Card Holder Name_____Card Issue #_____

   Signature _____Day Phone_____

☐ **BILL ME:** *(U.S. institutional orders only. Purchase order required.)*

   Purchase order # _____
   Federal Tax ID 13559302 • GST 89102-8052

Name_____

Address_____

Phone_____ E-mail_____

Copy or detach page and send to: **John Wiley & Sons, One Montgomery Street, Suite 1200,
San Francisco, CA 94104-4594**

Order Form can also be faxed to: **888-481-2665**

PROMO JBNND

CPSIA information can be obtained at www.ICGtesting.com
Printed in the USA
BVOW06s0249150715

408631BV00018B/253/P